TO THE
FAR CORNERS

*Including Excerpts
from
Billy Graham's Diary*

TO THE
FAR CORNERS

With Billy Graham in Asia

GEORGE BURNHAM

FLEMING H. REVELL COMPANY

Westwood, N. J.—316 Third Avenue
London E.C.4—29 Ludgate Hill
Glasgow C.2—229 Bothwell Street

CONTENTS

6 *Contents*

INTRODUCTION

During our recent trip to India and the Far East, we were privileged to see the greatest response to the message of the gospel we have ever witnessed. You had to be there to see it to believe it. Can you imagine 100,000 people in the heart of India's southern jungle listening to the gospel? Can you visualize people walking 400 and 500 miles to attend religious services? We saw miracles happen in city after city and country after country.

George Burnham graphically reported for hundreds of newspapers the thrilling stories of this tour. While Mr. Burnham has recorded his own observations and impressions and his opinions are his own, yet his reports of the meetings are authentic, thrilling, and moving. Millions have read his moving accounts of God at work. Through these pages you can go with us on this trip for which so many prayed. We must give God all the glory and acknowledge that it was His doing and not ours!

BILLY GRAHAM

Montreat, North Carolina

This book is dedicated to God, who provided the opportunity and the words. I would also like to dedicate it to my dear wife, Laura, and our wonderful children, Lynn, George, Jr., and John.

Grateful appreciation is given to Dr. Billy Graham, members of his team, and the newspaper for which I work, The Chattanooga News-Free Press.

GEORGE BURNHAM

FOREWORD

Only God could have made this book possible.

On December 30, two weeks before my scheduled departure for the Far East with Dr. Billy Graham, I was lying on a hospital bed in Chattanooga. Dr. Doyle Currey had just performed a major stomach operation.

"I'm afraid your trip is off, George," he said.

But Dr. Currey is an unusual man. He is a man of God first and a doctor of medicine second. He had found Christ, in a real way, three years before, after having been an officer in his church and teacher of an adult Sunday school class. The big change came when he noticed what Gideon Bibles did in the lives of his patients at the clinic.

The next morning after my operation he had several members of the Gideon Camp hold their regular Saturday morning prayer meeting in my room. They prayed that if it was God's will, that He would speed up the usual postoperative recovery, usually lasting about a month, and make it possible for me to make the trip.

A total of 600 newspapers, with a daily circulation of about 90,000,000 had signed up to run the series of stories from the Far East. To Dr. Currey and the Gideons, this looked like too much of an opportunity to be passed up, without appealing to the Great Physician.

The doctor is the kind of Christian who believes in putting feet to his prayers. On the first day he pulled me out of bed and made me walk around the room. I thought he was killing me, but next day it was easier. He knew what he was doing. Between hikes, he gave me cholera shots for the Far East.

On January 11 I flew to Atlanta for a yellow fever shot. This had to be given at a U. S. Public Health office.

On January 14 I flew to New York and when the plane sped down the runway at Idlewild next day I was on it. God had answered prayer, and He continued to answer prayer during the entire tour. I didn't have so much as a bad cold on the entire trip.

God had begun answering prayer in my life five years before, when I was an alcoholic reporter on a greased slide to oblivion. He picked me up out of the dust one night when I interviewed a preacher, Dr. Fred Garland.

Every story in this book was preceded by prayer. If they are good stories, the credit must go to Him.

To God be the glory; Great things He hath done!

GEORGE BURNHAM

Chattanooga, Tennessee

TO THE
FAR CORNERS

A PROMISE

Dr. Billy Graham, a thirty-seven-year-old evangelist who has spoken to more people in person than any man who ever lived, was quiet and thoughtful as he moved about the hotel room in New York.

He was to leave shortly for the longest trip of his life—a tour around the world, with speaking engagements in India, Thailand, the Philippines, Hong Kong, Formosa, Korea, Japan, and Hawaii. He also considered the trip to be the most important of his life, a life that had included triumphal tours of Scotland, England, and major countries of Europe.

This journey was going to be a little different from the others. The talented team that usually traveled with him was not going to be along. Soloist George Beverly Shea, with Paul Mickelson at the organ and Tedd Smith at the piano, would not be present to prepare the mood of the crowds before he spoke. He was taking only the message.

Billy walked into the hotel bathroom to check the dryness of a shirt he had washed the night before, in order to have everything clean for the 35,000-mile trip. He asked if the two thermos bottles had been filled. It was his intention to drink fresh American water forty-eight hours later in Bombay, India, the point from where all water would have to be boiled twenty minutes before it was safe to drink.

John Bolten of Andover, Mass., a prominent businessman who was going along on the trip to "pray and witness," entered the room. He had just arrived from Boston.

"Billy," he said, "I have a promise from God for you. It was telephoned to me at the airport by Dr. (Harold) Ockenga (pastor of Boston's Park Street Church, where Bolten is a lay leader). The verse was God's promise to Joshua after the death of Moses: 'As I was with Moses, so I will be with thee' " (Joshua 3:7).

Billy listened and then glanced out the window at the skyscrapers of Manhattan. His eyes moistened as he said, with quiet assurance, "Yes, as God was with us in Scotland, London, Paris, and Berlin, so will He be with us in India."

The events that followed proved his faith to be justified.

On the ride to Idlewild's International Air Terminal, Billy let his mind wander over happenings of the last few days. He thought about the conference he had been summoned to earlier in the week by Secretary of State Dulles. He had been briefed on American foreign policy concerning India and the Far East. Controversial Goa had been discussed. During the talk Mr. Dulles had said that the great need in the church today was a message of authority. He indicated that in some instances the American church had watered down the Bible message until it no longer had the appeal to the masses it once had.

Billy assured the Secretary of State that he was not taking a watered-down message to the Orient.

He said he intended to preach the same, simple messages he had always preached.

The airliner did a bit of wandering about the Atlantic. The pilot was bucking strong headwinds and was not quite sure he had enough fuel for the crossing. He flew within sight of Iceland in case a landing was necessary, but finally decided he had enough gas to reach Ireland.

A quick cup of coffee at the Shannon airport was proof that America and its comforts were far behind. Ireland has given many gifts to the United States, but a good cup of coffee was not among them. It tasted something like the oil drained from a crankcase.

The next stop was Paris. Fog covered the regular airport, but just a few miles away LeBourget was clear. This was the airport where Lindbergh landed on his fabulous flight in "The Spirit of St. Louis." LeBourget is now used as an alternate field.

An hour later the plane took off for Geneva, Switzerland, the beautiful city where Billy had preached several months earlier during the Big Four Summit Conference. One of the Trans-World airline officials there knew Billy was on board and had called members of the committee which had sponsored his previous visit. They came to the airport and told stories of people who had been converted at the Geneva meetings and were now living victorious Christian lives. The chairman said they had $600 left over after paying expenses of the services and only that week had sent it as a gift to Billy's "Hour of Decision" radio program.

Between stops, Billy read the Book of Ephesians and seemed to be refreshed by what he read.

Rome came into sight about midnight and then Athens about 3:00 A.M. It was the first time that Billy had ever been to Athens. He later wrote to his pretty wife, Ruth, back home in Montreat, N. C., with their four children: "It was clear, warm, and beautiful. I thought that I could spot Mars Hill, but I'm not sure. At least I used my imagination. There was a new thrill and sensation to coming into Athens, the place where the Apostle Paul had so many great experiences."

Shortly before dawn the plane approached Cairo. The pilot told Billy he would like to fly over the pyramids so he could see them but would have to come in high because of the touchy situations in the desert. Sometimes, he said, the trigger-happy herdsmen would shoot at the plane. He also said if he did not keep the proper course either Israeli or Egyptian fighter planes would come up and take a look at him.

During the short time in Cairo there was a lot of talk and thought in the small group about Moses, the bondage of the children of Israel, and the fact that Christ had been brought as a child to Egypt.

The sunrise came up over the Sinai Desert about fifteen minutes after the plane's departure. The Red Sea was crossed and then the plane came alongside Mt. Sinai, the place where God wrote with His finger the Ten Commandments on tablets of stone.

The engines were slowed by the pilot as a gesture

to Billy. There was a little white cloud hovering over the top of the mountain. As the sun splashed into it with a thousand colors Billy said he could imagine Moses standing there talking to God.

Down below was the desert where the children of Israel wandered for so many years. It was nothing but mile after mile of waste—canyons, ravines, nothingness.

"No wonder they had to be fed with manna from heaven," commented Billy. "No wonder they had to have water come from a rock. No wonder some of the people rebelled and wanted to go back to Egypt."

Later in the day the plane landed at Dhahran in Saudi Arabia. Outside the airport terminal, a member of the Moslem faith knelt in the dust and faced toward Mecca. It was a fresh reminder to Billy of why he had come.

Then, after more than forty hours in the air, the plane reached Bombay, India. Hundreds of people were gathered at the airport. They were singing hymns as Billy got off the plane. Their friendly, cheerful faces were in sharp contrast to the city beyond the airport—a dirty city of intrigue, hate, bitterness, and death.

CITY OF HATE

Billy Graham, who flew 8,000 miles to India as a representative of the Prince of Peace, was welcomed with a bloody orgy of mob violence described by newspapers as the blackest days in the history of ancient Bombay.

The visit by Billy was not the reason for the riots. They were caused by friction between two classes over the re-division of Indian states to relieve the tangled language situation. The people of India speak many dialects, with people living twenty miles apart unable to understand each other.

Billy just happened to arrive at the wrong time.

Armed mobs roamed the streets. Those without guns had clubs and rocks. People were killed, buses were burned, and cars were stoned by howling people racing through the streets . . . pillaging, plundering, stoning, hurting. Police opened fire on the mobs countless times, wounding hundreds and killing scores. And the officers were killed in return. One policeman was stoned to death at his post. Acid bombs were thrown into the faces of people. Angry men swarmed up and down side streets. They seemed to be without reason, lashing out at friend or foe. It was a city of human hate.

A young fellow with a stone in his hand was asked by Billy:

"Why are you throwing stones?"

He replied:

"I don't know. Somebody told me to."

Authorities agreed that the riots were inspired by Communists, who brought in goon squads.

Billy saw young men whipping an old shopkeeper because he wouldn't close his store. Several officers were killed when an armed mob invaded a police precinct station. The Billy Graham committee, checking on possibilities of carrying through with plans for a big open-air meeting, had left the station only minutes before.

The rally, which had enough reservations to assure it of being the largest Protestant religious meeting ever held in Bombay, had to be canceled. Two persons were killed outside the stadium where the meeting was scheduled to be held.

Over fifty people were killed during the week.

The week of violence brought to mind a statement Billy had made on many occasions:

"Our problems come from within, not without. An intellectual pilot will fly through the skies and drop an atom bomb on human beings. A jungle savage will creep along the trail and plunge a spear into a man. Why do these things happen? They happen because the human heart is wicked and will stay that way until it is transformed by the power of Jesus Christ. I believe that if peace is to come to the world and people are to live without fear of wars, it will only be through spiritual revival."

During his travels around Bombay, Billy saw other

things strange to an American. He saw a mongoose
kill a cobra, saw scores of starving mothers and fathers sleeping in the streets and then saw them tie
their few possessions to the branches of trees during
the day. He talked with educated Hindus who said
they would never kill a cow or an ant or any living
things for fear they would be killing an ancestor.

He saw other results of Hinduism—the pagan worship of over 30,000 assorted gods ranging from animals
to the crests of hills.

He saw the funeral of a Hindu. The man who had died
was old. With much ceremony, his body was placed
on a pile of wood. And then the eldest son put flowers
on top of the wood covering the body. Then he took
rice and other vegetables, turned his back and put it
down so the evil spirits couldn't see him doing it. He
ignited the wood with a torch. When only the bones
remained, the son took a stick and punched a hole in
the skull to free the spirit of his father. Mournful
Indian music was played in the background.

Billy heard about another sect of the Hindus, the
Parsis, who do not burn their bodies, but lay them out
in the temple. Vultures come down. In a few minutes
they strip all flesh from the body. The bones are then
consumed by fire.

When Billy returned to his hotel room after seeing
the violence and witnessing the rites of the Hindus,
he fell on his knees and prayed:

"Oh, God, help us to love these people. Help us
to put our arms around them and love them as Christ
would have done."

• • • • • •

Billy's Diary:

"Beggars were all around in Bombay—some men with their legs gone, others with their arms that had been eaten by disease, and blind men everywhere, all asking for money. It was one of the most heartbreaking scenes that I had seen since I left Korea. I wanted to give every one of them the message of Christ and give them all money. I did give some of them money.

"The missionaries and others, and even the Indian leaders, had warned us already not to give money, because every time you gave a rupee (which is worth about twelve cents and is also a day's wage in India) you would attract a thousand others because the word gets out quickly that you are giving money away. It's a most difficult thing to turn your back on such poverty as this. Some of them may be able to do it, but I can't. I gave as many rupees as I possibly could to as many people as I saw in need. However, the missionaries and Indian leaders were right—we soon collected a great crowd who were begging and screaming and fighting for money. We hastily got in our car and drove off."

CLOUDY PICTURE

Vital India, throbbing giant of the Far East and generally regarded as the key to all southeastern Asia, has been courted by world spokesmen from many lands.

But the courtship has grown lukewarm, as far as India's feelings for the United States are concerned.

America has spent millions in an effort to win favor with India's 400,000,000 people, more than twice the population of the U. S., in a land half the size. In spite of this, American popularity has been on the decrease. Secretary of State Dulles has been denounced loudly and often because of his views on Goa, an island just off the coast of India.

Russia's Bulganin and Khrushchev made a triumphal tour of India in 1955. They gained many followers. The Bombay riots were attributed to Communist agitation.

It was into such a picture as this that Billy stepped:

Religion, as such, does not present the answer, he stated. India may be the most religious nation on earth. A majority of the people are associated with the Hindu, Brahman, or Moslem religions.

Billy said he had come to present Jesus Christ as the only God and the only hope of the world.

He expressed the opinion, however, that if revival came to India, it would begin among the long-established group of Christians. There are about 10,000,000 Christians in India, with about half of them among the Roman Catholic faith.

When wild beasts and savages were roaming the hills in America, there were thriving Protestant churches in India.

Tradition says that Thomas, one of the twelve disciples, made a missionary journey to Cranganore, India, in 52 A.D. He was supposed to have established seven churches on the Malabar coast. Mar Thoma Church is thought to be an offshoot of the journey by Thomas.

Other Protestant groups are the Church of South India and the Jacobites. Two-thirds of the Christians in India are in the south, which corresponds to the "Bible Belt" of America.

A Protestant leader stated: "The church in India is the largest on the continent of Asia. Tens of thousands of these individual Christians, however, are members of churches whose history over the past few centuries is filled with intrigue, introversion, and indifference. Thousands more are but nominal Christians; adherents rather than believers. The giant church remains a bond slave, grinding at the mills of those to whom she should be declaring the unsearchable riches of Christ."

On the brighter side of Billy's visit were thousands of concerned Christians who prayed for several years that God would send him here. They put feet to their prayers with over 3,000 letters asking him to come. When he accepted the invitation for a three-week tour, Christians started a chain of twenty-four hour prayer meetings that God would do something big for India.

They had faith . . . about the size of a mustard seed.

• • • • • •

Billy's Diary:

"When leaving the hotel in Bombay, it becomes an immediate problem in tipping. We heard about one man that left the hotel, and eighteen men had lined up to get his tip. It seemed that people came from everywhere, people I hadn't even seen before, expecting a tip of some sort.

"Here in India there is so much unemployment that they employ several people to do one man's job in order to give a partial wage to as many people as possible, so you have many people waiting on you hand and foot wherever you go; whereas in America one man would handle the baggage, here five or ten will handle the baggage. In the hotels it is almost like it is on board ship, you have your cabin boy who is at your beck and call continually to bring you anything you want."

HOTEL LOBBY SERMON

The Taj Mahal hotel lobby in Bombay was in the process of coming to life. It was 6:00 A.M. The desk clerk was sleepy. Indian porters were shuffling about in their white sack trousers and tough bare feet.

Billy Graham strolled into the lobby. He had to catch an early plane to fill his busy schedule.

Four ladies, three white and one Indian, were standing off to one side. They approached Billy rather nervously and introduced themselves as missionaries, one from Canada, one from the United States and one from Great Britian. They had come from the Poona District, several hundred miles away.

"We rode an old broken-down train for two days to hear you speak," one said, "but it had engine trouble and did not arrive in time. Would you give us a brief message now that we might take it back to our people?"

She told Billy that a Sunday school class, composed of aged women and named the House of Peace, had been praying for many months that God would bless his meetings in India.

"They sold their extra rice and sent ten rupees (about $2.00) to help pay expenses of the meetings," she said.

Visibly touched by such self-sacrifice, Billy pulled out his Bible and began one of his most unusual and impressive services. He read, beginning at II Thessalonians 1:3:

"We are bound to thank God always for you, brethren, as it is meet, because that your faith groweth exceedingly, and the charity of every one of you all toward each other aboundeth.

"So that we ourselves glory in you in the churches of God for your patience and faith in all your persecutions and tribulations that ye endure. . . ."

Then Billy remarked:

"God will honor your faith and your sacrifice as you spend your lives in dark places of the world, taking the living message of Jesus Christ to hungry people. The things you suffer now will be as nothing when we meet the Master face to face. Don't let anything stop you from telling this wonderful story of God's love and grace."

By this time a fairly large crowd had gathered. The porters had stopped their shuffling to listen. The desk clerk was no longer sleepy. There had never before been a church service in his lobby before dawn.

All bowed their heads when Billy began to pray. One of the things he prayed for was that God would make him worthy to minister unto such devoted saints.

"God bless you," he said as he shook hands with each one of the missionaries.

He climbed into the bus for the ride to the airport.

And the workers in the hotel lobby went about the business of getting ready for another day.

SIDEWALK INCIDENT

The American had borrowed an Indian musical instrument and was trying to tame a cobra. His wife was focusing her camera to get the picture for the folks back home.

But the cobra didn't co-operate. He struck at the man. The American didn't run. He reached down quickly and got a strong grip on the cobra's head. The venom may have been removed from the snake's fangs, but it still took courage to grab him.

The wife wasn't quite so brave. She was shaking so badly that focusing a camera was out of the question. Dr. Bob Pierce of Los Angeles, a missionary pioneer in the Far East who was looking on with Billy Graham, stepped up and took the picture for her.

After the sidewalk incident the man introduced himself to Bob and Billy. He was Judge Philip B. Gilliam of Denver, Colo. Another bystander, who just happened to be on the scene, was the Rev. Reuben K. Youngdahl of Minneapolis. An American bull session developed on the street in Bombay.

Judge Gilliam was elected president of the National Council of Juvenile Court Judges in 1953. He was elected judge of Denver's famous juvenile court in 1940, and re-elected in 1944, 1948, and 1952, each time with the highest vote ever given any candidate for public office in the city and county of Denver. In these elections he received more votes than Roosevelt, Truman, or Eisenhower.

Certainly a representative American, he was in India making addresses as a delegate of the U. S. Information Service. He had heard about Billy Graham but had never heard him speak. During the next two days, he sat in on a press conference conducted by the evangelist and then, with his wife, attended a church service. They sat on the front row.

"I had heard a few of America's hellfire and damnation preachers and thought Mr. Graham might be another one," commented Mrs. Gilliam. "But he wasn't like that at all. He explained the fact of sin, the cure for it through faith in Jesus Christ, and then gave a common sense appeal for the people to make a decision on whether they would accept Christ or reject Him. There was nothing emotional about it. I was so impressed."

The judge added:

"Billy didn't appeal to the emotions, but my wife and I sat there with tears in our eyes. We have been church members for years, but I believe we will be better church members after hearing Billy. I believe that I will be a better judge when I return to Denver. As I sat there listening to this clean-cut young American I couldn't help wishing that every juvenile delinquent who appeared before me in the last twenty years could have heard him. He had the answer to their problems.

"Now that I have heard him and have seen the effect he has on people, I don't think there is a single man in the United States who can do as much for America abroad as Billy Graham."

That's quite a statement, but it comes from a successful American who can be regarded as a thoroughly reliable source.

Other competent statemen and newspapermen in Great Britain and Europe have said the same thing.

Billy's reply to all such praise, however, is always this:

"To God be the glory. Great things He hath done!"

PRESS CONFERENCE

Reporters were lounging around the room in Bombay firing questions at Billy Graham. Mob violence was taking place just a few blocks away. The fact that a press conference was under way was unusual, since reporters had rather write about fighting than preaching. But the most unusual thing about this press conference was the type of questions asked. The reporters didn't ask about Russia, Secretary of State Dulles, politics, or segregation.

A writer started it off with this question:

"What must a person do to become a Christian?"

And Billy answered:

"First of all, you must acknowledge that you are a sinner and be willing to renounce your sins. Then you must believe by faith that Jesus Christ is the Son of God and that He paid for your sins by dying on the cross. But that's not all. You must invite Him into your heart, humble yourself, and surrender your will to Christ. The Bible says if you confess your sins, God is faithful and just to forgive you for your sins and to cleanse you from all unrighteousness."

Almost before he had finished with the answer, another writer popped up with this one:

"What is sin?"

"Sin is the breaking of God's moral laws. If you break one of the Ten Commandments, you are a sinner. I have broken them. If you fail to live up to the Sermon on the Mount, you sin. I have failed to do this. Jesus Christ lived a perfect life, without sin. If you fail to live as good as Jesus, you are a sinner. I have never lived a day when I was as good as Jesus Christ. Have you? The Bible teaches that all have sinned and come short of the glory of God. The Bible says we are born in sin and then are sinners by choice."

Another question:

"What happens when a person dies?"

The answer:

"You have a body, with arms, legs, hands, nose, and feet. When you die, your body goes to the grave. But you are more than a body. You are a living soul, created in the image of God. Your soul will never die, according to the Bible. The Bible says that the soul of the Christian, at death, will immediately go into the presence of God and will remain with Him forever. The soul that dies without Christ will be cast into outer darkness, separated from God, in a place that Jesus called hell."

Then a reporter asked this:

"What happens when a little child dies? You said they were born in sin. Would a just God punish them?"

Billy answered:

"I believe the Bible teaches that all children who die before they reach the age of accountability will go to heaven."

Another queried:

"How can a person know that he has eternal life with God?"

The answer: "The Bible says, 'He that hath the Son hath life; he that hath not the Son hath not life.' It is a matter of faith. Faith goes beyond understanding. Surrender your will to Christ and you will know in your heart that you are a child of God. You will lose your fear of death. You will have a smile on your face. You will go out and begin to live the Christian life."

Many other questions were asked along the same line and all were answered with "the Bible says. . . ."

The reporters were milling around in the room after the conclusion of the press conference when one of them walked up to Billy, stuck out his hand, and said:

"I want to become a Christian. Will you show me how?"

The reporter had a smile on his face when he went out the door.

FACES OF PEOPLE

The outmoded twin-engine plane sat near the terminal in Bombay, ready for passengers and the five-hour flight across country to the port city of Madras in southern India.

It wasn't the type of plane a person would choose if he had a choice. But in India there was no choice— it's the Indian Airline or none at all. And India may be the only country in the world that will not honor air credit cards. Hard cash is the only acceptable currency.

Any person who doesn't care for such dictatorial treatment at the hands of an airline can always take the train. The run from Bombay to Madras requires only about four days. It can be made by private car, but plenty of provisions should be stocked beforehand. Some of the roads are like the wagon trails during the settling of the west. Others are partially paved and impartially bumpy.

Desolate country, for the most part, flowed past the wing tips of the plane. Splotches of what appeared to be stale, putrid water occasionally dotted the landscape. Always located near the priceless water were clusters of thatch-roofed houses. Mountain ridges soared upwards at grotesque angles. It looked like rugged living. The land was poor, producing little food.

There seemed to be a different atmosphere in Madras. It was an intangible substance, but could be easily felt. This was one of India's centers of Christianity. The faces of the people seemed to be different, even though they had the same dark color as those in Bombay.

Writing in his diary, Billy said this about the faces:

"It was a thrilling sight to see these Indians with their shining white teeth and open, friendly faces, many of them spirit-filled men who have suffered much in the name of Christ. What a difference there is between the Christian in India and the average man on the street! The average man seemingly has a fairly hard, morbid look on his face. Yet the Christian is so completely different. If I didn't believe in Christ, I would believe in Him from that point alone—what He does to the faces of people. They are just as different as day and night!"

During the few days in Madras, we had become acquainted with the Indian crows, but it was in Madras that the acquaintance became overbearing. There were thousands of them. The Indians seemingly never kill anything, for fear it might be their grandmother born again as an animal.

Squawking loudly and often, the crows would come into the hotel room, eat the fruit, and pick up any bright object, like a tie clasp or money clip, that happened to be lying around. One morning, as I was typing a story, a crow flew in and landed on the back of my chair. Every time I turned around he would retreat to the balcony, but as soon as I resumed

typing he would return to the chair. Occasionally, I
imagined that the Peeping Tom gave disapproving
squawks at what he read.

• • • • • •

The food in southern India was not as good as that
in Bombay, and the food in Bombay was not anything
to write home about . . . so I did very little eating and
no writing home about it at all.

My diet, which I was laughingly supposed to be
on after a pre-trip operation, consisted mostly of pa-
paya, pineapple, rice and chicken currie, plus a sampl-
ing of mutton at practically every meal. For some
reason the goats have never gotten around to attaining
much of a godly status in the Hindu religion. They
bleated about it, but to no avail.

A majority of the economic problems now suffered
in India could be wiped out overnight if they would
eat their cows instead of worshiping them. Probably,
there would be at least one cow for each of the 400,-
000,000 people, with a calf left over for dessert. This
will never be, however. Mahatma Gandhi once said
the worship of the cow was the one thing that held
India together.

Several Hindus were spotted one day out in a stream
of water giving a bath to a cow god. They scrubbed
her from stem to stern for about forty-five minutes.
The cow would try to break away, but they would
haul her back and scrub some more. Old Betsy appeared to be about the most miserable god that ever

lived. There is no doubt that she would have given up all her heavenly glory for a quiet pasture well away from the icy fingers of her faithful subjects.

• • • • • •

During Billy's visit to Germany in 1955, he tried many times to meet Lutheran Bishop Hans Lilje of Hanover, one of the world's most influential church figures. But he was never successful because of conflicting dates.

In January, 1956, however, Billy was walking into the lobby of the Connemara Hotel in southern India. He accidently bumped into a man near the entrance. It was Bishop Lilje.

"God works His wonders in mysterious ways," they agreed.

• • • • • •

Billy's Diary:

"You will be interested in the reaction of the audience to the preaching. It's very much like an English audience. They catch on to humor and other things very readily and very quickly. They have keen minds. And when I told a little bit of humor, they would laugh three times—those in English and those in the other two languages."

• • • • • •

Billy's Diary:

"This afternoon we saw a heart-breaking sight. I didn't actually see it, but Jerry told me about it. The little mail clerk at the desk has been so sweet and kind and friendly. He goes out of his way to help us in every way he possibly can. Three braggadocious, swaggering, tipsy American tourists came in. Within a few minutes they had the whole lobby upset by their cursing and swearing at this dear little man. If I'd been down there, I am sure that I would have gone up and rebuked them.

"These are the types of American tourists that are giving us a bad name and making people hate us all over the world. These are the types of tourists whose passports I would be in favor of canceling. These people in Madras are genuinely friendly to Americans, hungry for our friendship, and doing everything they can to please. Then some rich, braggadocious, half-drunk American tourists come in and spoil it all. If I ever became President of the United States, I would revoke every passport of every tourist reported to be misbehaving."

• • • • • •

Billy's Diary:

"Had an hour today with Mr. Bashsingh, the great Indian evangelist who has established 300 congregations in India. He is completely indigenous, does not accept money from Europe or America, and is entirely self-supporting. He apparently is teaching the Indian Church that it can stand on its own feet. However, he is not well received in many of the main line denominations, such as the Church of South India. They consider him rather divisive; they claim that many of his members come from some of their congregations. However, they all admit that God is with him and that he has a powerful and ringing testimony. He is a Sikh from up in Punjab—handsome, yellow skinned, well educated. He studied in London; then on his way to Canada to work in the wheat fields during the summer, he was marvelously converted on a ship in a Christian service. He answered the call to preach while in Canada and came back to India and has been used mightily of God ever since."

HUNGRY PEOPLE

Among many thousands of people who poured into Madras from all parts of India to hear Billy Graham was one man who walked over 400 miles. He preached at villages along the way.

When told about the man, Billy replied, "I am not worthy of preaching to that man. I should be sitting at his feet."

One hundred people from Hyderabad, 800 miles away, rode a train four days and nights. They had been praying in a twenty-four-hour prayer chain for weeks that God would bless India through Billy.

When all accommodations in town were gone, people went from house to house seeking rooms. Hundreds slept in the open. They had come to hear a man who had the peculiar talent for talking about God in a language that people could understand.

Morning meetings at 7:00 o'clock and evening meetings at 6:00 o'clock were scheduled for three days. The morning meetings were held for ministers, with more than 5,000 on hand at dawn for the first meeting.

Over 30,000 turned out for the evening rally. Some of the people sat at the site all day. About 3,000 were present by 2:00 P.M. Billy has had larger crowds, but there was something different about this one. People, some dressed in rags and others in the finest of silk robes, sat on grass mats and waited. Most were barefooted. Men and women never sit together in church. There was no hum of conversations. People were quiet. It was an unreal quietness.

There were two choirs of 300 each. One sang in English, the other in Indian dialect. An Indian band played music which had a foot-patting beat to it.

Billy stepped up to the microphone. He had two interpreters instead of the usual one. The message had to be translated into Telegu and Tamil languages. He would stop after each phrase or sentence and had plenty of time to scratch his head before time to speak again.

Billy spoke about a man by the name of Jesus Christ. Some of the people in the strange congregation had never before heard of Him. To others, Christ was just one of thousands of other gods, but Billy described Him as the only God, with the Bible quotation: "I am the way, the truth and the life. No man cometh unto the Father but by me."

He added:

"Many Indians seem to have the idea that Christianity is a western religion. That is wrong. There were Christian churches in India before America was discovered. Christ was an easterner. His skin was not as light as mine and it was not as dark as yours." A wire service dispatch quoted Billy as saying Christ was a Negro. He did not say that.

He described Christ as the only road to heaven and then told eager listeners they could only get there by repentance of sin and receiving Jesus by faith.

He gave the invitation. The response was immediate. The front aisle was filled in minutes. Some of those standing before the platform wore a tiny dot in the forehead—the sign of a Hindu holy man. A man knelt with his face in the dust. Pitiful little children with their ribs showing stood there looking up. Members of the high and low castes stood side by side. The front aisle became dangerously crowded and Billy had to ask people to stand in the back passages. In the counseling room a total of 1,389 signed decision cards. But over 4,000 Gospels of John were given out. There were not enough Tamil, Telegu, and English counselors to go around.

On the second night 904 signed cards and over 1,000 signed decision cards the third night.

Probably the most impressive service of the Madras meetings was a morning address to 7,000 students of the area. Billy stressed the folly of rejecting Christ because the human mind cannot understand all about Him intellectually.

Two hundred and fifty of the students responded to the invitation. A missionary in India for many years said, "These are the finest young men and women in India. This is the first time anyone has ever reached their hearts with the gospel of Christ." His eyes were filled with tears.

During three days in Madras Billy spoke to over 100,000 Indians and recorded about 4,000 decisions for Christ. Bulganin and Khrushchev didn't do as well.

Pathetic, half-starved people were seen bringing

their offerings of fruits and other foodstuffs to the gods in one of the Hindu temples at Madras.

A priest would take the offering inside to see if it was acceptable. The gods, for some reason, never refused to take the offering.

There was a great contrast between the fat, sleek-looking priests and the underfed people. And servants of the priests invariably were the nicest looking young girls to be found in India.

● ● ● ● ● ●

Billy's Diary:

"Went out to the beach this morning and spent about an hour and a half. The little children soon came around us, most of them were practically naked, but they were about as cute and sweet as anything I've ever seen. They were as black as ebony, but had happy, sweet expressions on their faces. The little girls all have their noses punctured, with jewelry in the nose and in the ears. The little girls also have a lot of gold- or brass-looking ornaments on their arms.

"One little boy that we liked especially did all sorts of little dances for us. He could make all of his bones in his body crack. His arms and legs were very skinny from malnutrition, sores were on his back—he was a pitiful, yet lovable sight. As soon as we went back to the taxi, we gave two or three of them a rupee each. They went wild! People began running from everywhere. It seems that word travels swiftly and we had to get out quickly or would have been mobbed with people wanting money. We were beginning to learn that it's a dangerous thing to give money publicly like that to anyone."

• • • • • •

Billy's Diary:

"The driver took us over to one of the great Hindu temples to watch the worshipers. Jerry and I took off our shoes and went inside. We got the surprise of our lives. It was a temple to Siva, and part of the worship of Siva is phallic worship, which is the worship of the reproductive organs of the male. Here we saw the priests offering vegetables, et cetera, to the god, and the people lined up outside, many of them prostrate, praying to God. When their particular sacrifice has been offered, the priest comes back and offers camphor ashes which are put on the forehead of the worshiper, indicating that his sacrifice is accepted by the god. Then we went into an inner court, and there was a small lake—stagnant, dirty water. Steps were going down to the lake, completely around the lake. It would have cost millions of dollars in America to build such an extensive temple with all of its various manifestations of Siva and this huge lake of stagnant rain water. Hundreds of people were washing their clothes, others were bathing, and others were drinking. It was considered holy water. It was almost impossible to believe our eyes. We stood and watched it and almost wept, longing that these people might know the forgiveness that is in Christ. How they could

possibly live after drinking that filthy water, I don't
know."

● ● ● ● ● ●

Billy's Diary:

"On the way into town I had opportunity to observe
the endless stream of people again, to watch the
women as they would carry huge loads on their heads
—certainly the woman in India is still, in one sense,
a beast of burden. I've never seen women work as
they do here; not even in Switzerland or Germany
have I seen them do such heavy work as they are doing here in India. We watched them as they did their
laundry in the riverbed. They take the clothes and
beat them over stones and boulders until the dirt apparently comes out. Woe be to any buttons."

SERMON ON MOUNT

People who gathered to hear Christ preach the Sermon on the Mount must have looked something like the 100,000 who sat on the hillsides at Kottayam to hear Billy Graham. This is not an attempt to compare the two speakers. The people are the story.

Billy stood on a platform in the center of a clearing. People covered the hillside all around him. Almost as far as the eye could see it was a sea of white, dotted with splashes of color, that rose and fell with the levels of the hills. The women were dressed in their billowing white robes and the men attired in loose fitting clothes that defy description. It appeared that men got tangled up in a sheet while getting out of bed and then wore it that way the rest of the day. Americans would be more comfortable if they dressed like the people of India. They dress for weather, not to impress people.

The listeners had come from miles around. They were of all ages—young boys who couldn't sit still, mothers with little children, aging parents whose faces reflected hard years of working fields. There were Jacobites with long beards.

Kottayam has a population of about 50,000. Billy's service doubled it. The other thousands walked ten to twenty miles from the surrounding countryside. After arriving at the meeting, they thanked God for a full moon. The light helped them to see the deadly cobras along the dense jungle trails. Americans wouldn't walk ten miles to church along a paved sidewalk in broad daylight.

The Indians had heard of this outstanding young preacher from the other side of the world and had been planning for many months to hear him speak. It was a mood of expectancy as they looked toward the platform.

Billy began to speak through a Malayan interpreter. A few days before it was in Tamil and Telegu. He said, "God is going to do big things at these meetings in southern India. He is not going to do them because I am a great preacher. I am not a great preacher. He is going to do these big things because Christians in India and your friends around the world have been praying. God answers prayers.

"The message I am going to preach is 2,000 years old, but it is as modern as tomorrow's newspaper. I will preach Jesus and Him crucified."

And that is what he preached—with simplicity, conviction, and power. It touched a lot of people in a lot of different ways. Preachers were brought together in a spirit of unity never before known in India. Missionaries from abroad said they were going back to their remote outposts with new zeal and a sense of urgency. Non-Christians responded by the thousands to the message of peace for the present and hope for the future.

"Only God could have done this," Billy commented. His thoughts, too, had drifted back to the Sermon on the Mount as he looked out over the people. Christ could not be seen, but many said they had felt His presence.

• • • • • •

Speaking through an interpreter has hidden disadvantages, along with the obvious. Some languages and dialects do not have words to give the exact meaning of the English used.

In his address to the 100,000 at Kottayam, Billy used a little humor in remarking about all the bugs flying around on the platform. The interpreter had no word for bugs. The closest he could come to it was "bedbugs," so he remarked about all the bedbugs flying around the platform.

A classic concerns the speaker in India who began by saying: "I'm tickled to death to be here." The interpreter thought for a minute and said: "Our speaker is so happy to be here that he has caught the itch and scratched himself to death."

• • • • • •

It was decided that Billy, Jerry Beavan, team public relations man, and Paul Maddox, personal aide, would stay at Bishop Jacob's house in Kottayam.

They didn't think too much of the idea, however, after the Bishop said snake charmers had captured twenty-six cobras in his yard the previous week. He comforted them by saying, "People are bitten every

day, but many of them live after the experience."
And, by way of further assurance, he said that cobras
rarely came into the house.

• • • • • •

Billy's Diary:

"After lunch, we proceeded in three cars from
Cochin to Kottayam. It took us about two-and-a-half
hours. It was one of the most interesting and hair-
raising experiences of my life. Bishop Jacob has a
driver by the name of Matthew. I had already been
warned by David Cowie and Bob Munger, who were
here two or three years ago, that Matthew was one
of the wildest drivers in all the world. I remember
Dave had to caution the Bishop that his wife just
could not take the driving of Matthew. We soon knew
what Dave and Bob were talking about.

"Matthew kept going from fifty to sixty miles an
hour over a road nine feet wide, absolutely jammed
with rickshas, carts, wagons, automobiles, people,
dogs, goats, and cows. He tooted the horn all the way.
The chickens, dogs, cows, and goats scrambled in
every direction. He would slam on the brakes at times,
jolting us to a sudden stop as a cow would cross our
path. I am sure that all night long tonight I will be
hearing the toot of that horn. On the other hand, it
was a beautiful trip. It was right down through some
of the most densely populated area in the world,
through a teeming jungle."

Billy's Diary:

"The Bishop took me over to the edge of his beautiful yard, and we looked down a cliff to behold one of the most beautiful and interesting sights I've ever seen. Out before us was an amphitheater that had been built largely for our meetings. It was in great terraces, row upon row. It would be able to accommodate from 100,000 to 200,000 people. It had been dug out by girls with baskets, working as a labor of love. A beautiful platform had been built in the middle. Fences had been built to put people in various congregations. Beyond that are the greenest rice paddies I've ever seen, and beyond that is the jungle."

• • • • • •

Billy's Diary:

"One of the interesting things is that when I leave the platform at night, the Bishop always takes me through the milling crowd. It's in a sense a terrifying experience with the crowd pressing in close with their dark faces peering at you, trying to get us in view; and you could imagine that anything could happen if they became excited. But the Bishop gives his commands and orders and the crowd moves as did the Red Sea before Moses. When the Bishop speaks, the people move, and he comes through, and we are trailing along behind him, sticking as closely as we possibly can to keep from getting crushed by the multitude."

"FRIGHTENING" REACTION

"This is frightening."

Dr. Robert Pierce, president of World Vision, Inc. and noted American missionary leader who has seen many strange sights in the Orient, breathed these words a few minutes after Billy Graham had given 40,000 Indians in Palamcottah an invitation to become Christians. It was clear that the scene was frightening in a wonderful way.

An estimated 4,000 surged toward the platform. There was not enough space to hold them. The average response from a crowd like this had been 1,000. Many believing Christians in the packed throng expected God to do something big, but few were prepared for the thousands who moved forward to accept this new way of life.

There was something in the faces of the people as they came. Many were weeping. Others had a look of joy. Both reactions had been produced by the same message.

Men and women, who had been sitting on straw mats in different sections of the huge outdoor meeting site, moved down the aisles and quickly filled the space around the platform. Still they rushed forward.

A blind man was led by his daughter. A worker had told the daughter she would have to send the father alone with the men, but Dr. Paul Maddox, Billy Graham's aide, intervened and told the daughter she could take him to the women's section.

A woman, sobbing quietly, left her seat and moved forward. She had gone only a short way when her angry husband rushed up and grabbed her roughly and pulled her from the stream of people.

The people were of all types—young and vigorous, old and ugly, deformed and diseased. There were only 400 counselors to talk with the 4,000.

When it became clearly dangerous for more people to come forward, Billy asked them to remain in the aisles. Many of them waited for hours until counselors had a chance to get their names and say a few words to them.

Church leaders said they should have expected something unusual at the end because "the devil did everything he could to break it up at the beginning."

The public address system failed and the spirited choir almost sang itself to death. A little boy was brought to the platform. Cliff Barrows said his mother was lost. Then Billy began his address. A few minutes later he had to stop when a great clamor went up from a section of the crowd. They couldn't hear, because of a faulty loudspeaker. As the people were moved to another section, Billy began again. He spoke simply— carefully explaining the way to God through faith in Christ. Then came the invitation and unexpected surge of people.

A missionary who had served in India for twenty-five years stood off to one side and looked on with choked emotions. He said: "Our eyes have never seen anything like this." His prayers had been answered. He said he had started the day by reading in Joshua 3:4 ". . . ye have not passed this way heretofore."

• • • • • •

Billy's Diary:

"It was a beautiful evening with another incomparable sunset. Then when the time came for me to get up to speak, there was great confusion over to my right. People began to shout and scream and jump up, and I could not figure out what was going on, so I stopped. This was the first interruption we have had during our entire tour, and I wasn't certain what it was about. I turned it over to Bishop Jabiraga and found out that the people over there could not hear. There was no amplification in that direction. Soon all was bedlam, everything was in confusion. Some of the European leaders thought that the crowd would get into a stampede and would start bolting and many people might be trampled. They say it was very easy for that to happen here. They began moving that end of the crowd around toward the back so they could get in front of the amplifiers. Down below there were about twenty people trying to run the amplification. Everybody was shouting at everybody else. On the platform the ministers were all in confusion. They were shouting words of advice to the Bishop. Some

were saying this and some were saying that. Yet all
the time there seemed to be a strange quietness and
hush in my heart. I knew somehow that God was going
to bring order. I reached over and put my arm around
the Bishop and told him not to worry. He seemed to
be very deeply concerned. I told him we had had
problems like this before and that it would all work
out. He got up to speak to the people to try to quiet
them. Then I bowed my head and prayed a prayer
that I have not prayed in a long time. It was almost
a prayer of commanding, a prayer of authority. I remember I opened my hand as though to come down
upon the crowd, and I said, 'Oh God, stop the noise;
quiet the people now.' Immediately a deathlike hush
came on the crowd, and it became the quietest, most
reverent meeting we have had in India yet. It was like
the breath of God had suddenly fallen. You couldn't
hear a sound.

"I preached for about an hour and had tremendous
power and liberty. I knew that the message of God
was going home. I felt that I could preach for another hour, but it was time to close, and when we
closed, I gave the invitation. Then Pentecost fell. People began to run forward and fall upon their knees.
Some of them began to scream to God for mercy;
others were saying, 'Jesus, save me. Jesus, save me,'
until about 3,000 to 4,000 people had come, and we
had to stop the invitation because there was no room
for anyone else. They were falling on their knees like
flies. It was almost as if they were being slain by the

Lord. The Bishop leaned over to me and said that he
saw a Hindu leader down on his knees with tears coming from his eyes, crying, 'Jesus, save me.'

"How we thank God for having just a little part in
this great movement of the Spirit. Certainly tonight's
demonstration of the Spirit is the deepest and greatest
that I have ever sensed. It is almost like something
you read about in the ministry of Charles Finney."

• • • • • •

Billy's Diary:

"Down here we are continually perspiring and taking baths. You should see me trying to take a bath
in the big tub. There is no tub as we know it, but there
is a big tub where you pour in the water and take a
bath. It reminds me of when I was a boy. That's the
way we took baths until we had an inside bathroom.
We would get in the round tub as children and all of
us take baths in the same tub. That's about the way
we are doing here."

• • • • • •

Billy's Diary:

"The first meeting I had today was a women's meeting. I was supposed to address the women at the
Cathedral. The Cathedral was jammed and some
5,000 or 6,000 people were jamming the outside, and
the streets were lined with people. People waved at
us as we went by, and as we got to the Cathedral, the

press of the crowd was so great that our car could not get through. The people were pressing and fighting. I almost thought the car would overturn, they were pushing it, grabbing. Many of them were trying to touch us, many of them were trying to touch the car. It has almost reached the point now of adulation, and Jack Dain (English missionary who planned the Indian trip) is fearful that many of the Hindus are beginning to accept me as a god. Many of them fall down and practically worship me as I come by. Many of them try to get in my shadow. I told them time after time, very much as Peter, that I am not a god but a man; but the word is spreading all over the southern part of India as to what God is doing, and people are coming for miles to see and hear the revival. Many have heard that revival is here and that God's message is being spoken and it travels by word of mouth, so today the ox carts are bringing in thousands of new people from the surrounding area. Some of them have come for a hundred miles. The missionaries, pastors, and bishops say there has never been anything like it in the history of the Christian Church in India."

● ● ● ● ● ●

Billy's Diary:

"Immediately after the service I bade good-by to Bishop Jabiraga, said good-by to the Burns, the Englands, and the others from Dohnavur and all of those that had made our stay in Palamcottah a never-to-be-forgotten experience. Bob Pierce rode in the car with me. We talked and ate oranges. They had packed lunches for us of sandwiches and boiled eggs, and we ate our lunches—and of course the everlasting banana was the main part of the lunch. I've eaten so many bananas until I feel like I'm going to turn into a banana. On the way down, ox carts filled the highway. Apparently people wait until it is cool in the evening and start driving their ox carts. I understand that many men will start their oxen down the road and then go to sleep, and the ox takes them to their destination. I have also heard stories of how the oxen may be going along at night, the man may be asleep, and for a prank some of the people will turn the oxen around. When the man wakes up the next morning, he finds that he is back where he started from."

NEHRU LISTENS

Prime Minister Nehru of India, who has described himself as Hindu by birth, Moslem by culture, and Christian by ethics, seemed a bit preoccupied at the beginning of his thirty-minute talk with Billy Graham in New Delhi.

Nehru had been holding a lot of conferences on world affairs and had talked with a lot of important foreigners. He might have been thinking about any number of world-shaking problems.

But he warmed up and was very gracious as he talked with the evangelist. The Prime Minister displayed an amazing knowledge of the Bible.

He said he was impressed by the story of the Good Samaritan but expressed the feeling that Christian nations too often have treated India as the priest and the Levite treated the victim. His antagonism, if any, was toward the behavior of Christian nations and not Christianity itself.

Nehru, son of a wealthy lawyer, spent fourteen years in jail in his fight for Indian freedom and he has been portrayed as a strong negotiator for world peace. It was on this point that he did a little listening to the young preacher.

Billy told him that the world respected him as a man of peace. But he added, "Peace conferences are no stronger than human nature and human nature is diseased. Despite all his culture, man continues to lie and steal and fight. In over 3,000 years of history there have been only 300 years of peace. Why? It is because man has rejected God's offer of peace through faith in His Son, Jesus Christ."

Billy added: "Christ can transform human nature. He transformed mine, and I have seen Him change the lives of thousands of others around the world." Billy gave Nehru his own testimony on the decision he made for Christ as a youth of sixteen.

He said:

"Before this decision to live for Christ, I didn't care anything about God, the Bible, or people. I was filled with intolerance, but the simple act changed my nature. I began to worship God and I loved people no matter what color their skin might be."

"Peace will come," he said, "when people turn by faith to Christ."

Nehru didn't say yea or nay along these lines, but Billy said later, "I had a very strong impression that he was pro-Christian."

India has taken restive measures against missionary activity, but it is believed this objection has been to foreign activity and not Christian activity. India wants people to come who will do something about providing its millions with homes, food, hospitals, and schools.

Crowds for Billy's meetings in Delhi were smaller, averaging around 10,000. Few Christians are residents of the north. Over 600 walked forward at each service,

the greatest percentage of decisions seen in India.
Many leaders of the government were present. Raj-
kumari Amrit Kaur, minister for health and close
friend of Nehru, presided at the opening service. Sitting on the platform were five ambassadors and two
queens.

People came from as far away as 1,200 miles. A
missionary group of 500 was living in a tent city in
order to attend.

Billy delivered a simple gospel message and gave
an invitation. People crowded to the front. The chairman of Graham's Delhi committee left his place on
the platform and stood with the converts. He went
to Billy in his hotel room after the meeting and said:
"I didn't know what the people might think if the
chairman of the committee admitted his life wasn't
right. But I didn't have peace in my soul and I had
to take my place before the platform. Now I have
peace."

· · · · · ·

An Indian Christian overheard a leading Indian
statesman say this to Bulganin and Khrushchev when
the Russians were in Madras: "You have made two
mistakes. You have left God out of your plan and you
use violence to accomplish your objectives. Being a
western nation, you should have accepted Jesus
Christ."

The quote isn't as remarkable as the fact that it was

made by a Hindu man who worships many gods. Bulganin was reported to have replied that Russia was now much more tolerant regarding religious worship.

• • • • • •

Billy's Diary:

"I was deeply touched by the reception at the airport in Delhi. Many of those people had been there for hours, waiting on us to come. What hospitality and friendliness these people exude! That's India. No wonder Khrushchev and Bulganin got such a welcome. I think the Indians would welcome anybody like that. If Eisenhower came to India, he would get the most overwhelming reception of his life, and it would do America a whale of a lot of good. They don't care two hoots for all the money we give them, but they are thrilled to death when we come in person to visit them."

• • • • • •

Billy's Diary:

"At 11:00 o'clock we went in to Mr. Nehru's office. He was talking to Mr. Dag Hammarskjold, and so we had to wait. About 11:15, Mr. Hammarskjold came out of Mr. Nehru's office. Mr. Hammarskjold is tall—I believe taller than I am—very handsome and very striking looking. Two or three men were with him. When he saw me, he paused a moment, looked in my direction, and then went on. I imagine that he thought he recognized me, or he had seen my picture somewhere,

and thought about speaking. I thought about going up
to him and introducing myself, but at that moment Mr.
Nehru's secretary called to me and said that the Prime
Minister could see us now. Bob Pierce was with me.

"We walked in about 11:18, and we stayed there for
about thirty-five minutes. Mr. Nehru got up from his
desk and greeted us very cordially. He said he was delighted to have us in India, and asked us to be seated.
We sat down and then he didn't say anything, so I told
him how much we respected him, how much many
Americans admired him, even though we did not agree
with all that he did and said. I said that I thought that
perhaps he had been misinterpreted by many Americans and that most Americans did not realize the
tremendous social, political, and economic problems
that he was faced with here in India. When I got
through what I considered a rather pleasant speech, he
didn't say anything. He just sat there with a letter-
opener in his hand, twiddling it.

"Then I decided that I would tell him about our
tour of India, so I told him all about it. He still didn't
say a word, and there was a dead silence for a moment.
I had never had an interview quite like it. And then I
decided I'd tell him what Christ had done for me, and
I told him in no uncertain terms what Christ had done
in my own life, how He had changed me and given me
peace and joy, and how He had forgiven my sins. Then
immediately he began to be interested. He began to
ask some questions. Then Bob Pierce began to ask him
about missionary work in India. Mr. Nehru gave us a
complete review of Christianity in India. He said that

Christianity came to India in three ways: first, in the first century led by Saint Thomas . . . that has become a great indigenous Indian Church that has been here for 2,000 years. Second, when the Portuguese came, they brought the Catholic Church. He said the Catholics were very shrewd, alert, and smart. He said they came in first to study, and they became great Sanskrit scholars. Then after they had been here for some years, they began to teach and practice their religion, and he said as a result, Catholicism is very strong in India. Then he said about 300 years ago the British came with their missionaries. And he said that the Anglican Church appealed to the Indian people almost as an imperial arm, a religious arm of the British government. And he said therefore the Anglican churches had been in some suspect by Indians as engaging in political activity. He thought that was now quite largely dissipated because the Anglican Church in the South had gone into the Church of South India. He thought that the Church of South India would become very soon an indigenous, self-supporting Indian Church. He thought that was very good.

"He said that the government was not against missionaries in India. He said, 'We welcome missionaries; they are doing a wonderful work.' But he said, 'We have had some missionaries, particularly in the North, where we have very sensitive areas, that have engaged in political activity,' and he said, 'That's something that the government will not stand for.' And he said that that had only been in a few cases. He cited one case in Burma where some missionaries had helped lead some riots against the government. He said that was very unfortunate, but he said that the Indian government was in no way against missionary activity. This was quite gratifying news, though after talking to many missionaries, I am finding that the consensus of opinion of missionaries in India is that unless the missionaries become integrated within the Indian Church and are working under Indian leadership that their influence in India is going to be very small, that the day is over when we can use early twentieth-century methods in winning the Indian to Christ, that the missionary and his compound is totally out of date, that the Indian Church is strong enough now that missionaries coming should work with and integrate into the Indian Church under Indian leadership. That is being done by most of the major denominations and is proving very satisfactory. And it's wonderful to see these European, British, and American missionaries under Indian leadership, and the Christian churches are beginning to develop rapidly their own leadership.

"Mr. Nehru, before we left, further commended us for coming. He said we were very welcome in India, and he thought we had done a good work; and he said that he thought that our work had helped to interpret America better to the Indian people. We left about noon."

CONCENTRATED JOY

Many memorable events have been packed into the life of Billy Graham. He has walked with kings and presidents, but probably the most moving experience of his life occurred in a comparatively unknown place near the southern tip of India.

The experience began with a letter from his wife. In the letter, waiting for him when he arrived at Palamcottah, she wrote that he was very near Dohnavur and said it would be a shame if he didn't get to visit the huge "family" made famous by the devoted life and inspired writings of Miss Amy Carmichael.

Miss Carmichael, who died in 1951 at the age of eighty-four after spending most of her life on the mission field, founded the home for unfortunate children of India in 1901. She was aided in the founding by the Rev. Thomas Walker, one of the most noted missionaries ever to work in Asia.

She began the work with one child—a child who had been dedicated by her parents to an immoral life in a Hindu Temple. In past years it was common practice for Hindu parents to promise the next child to the temple in return for an immediate blessing. The practice has now been forbidden by the government, but observers said it had not been stamped out. Miss Carmichael rescued every child she could. Today, Dohnavur is the world's largest family—with over 900 people.

It was Miss Carmichael's idea from the beginning that Dohnavur would be a "family" and not an institution. She saturated the work with prayer and love.

Billy said his wife had prayed many years for Dohnavur and had read every book ever written by Miss Carmichael. Some of the most famous were *God by Moonlight, Rose From Brier, If,* and *Lotus Buds.*

He made arrangements for the short trip. Immediately after addressing an overflow morning meeting of ministers at the Palamcottah Cathedral (he had to exit through a window), Billy departed by car on the thirty-two-mile trip to Dohnavur. Serving as his guide was Norman Burns, an Australian who has been a senior member of the family for twenty-four years.

The western Ghat Mountains could be seen in the distance, where the jagged peaks formed an impressive backdrop for the 400-acre home.

A picture of peace and beauty began to take shape several miles before the home was reached. Aged banyan trees lined each side of the road and cut off the scorching rays of the hot sun. To the side could be seen scores of rice fields, bordered by banana and coconut groves.

The car passed through the tiny village of Kalakad, which means Joyous City. A few miles farther was Dohnavur, a giant cluster of clean, cool, strong-looking buildings.

Word of Billy's visit had preceded him. The boys and girls, men and women, were as anxious to get a look at Billy as he was to get a look at Dohnavur.

First part to be visited was the girls' compound. There were big groups of the joyous little girls, all of whom were clean and pretty in their dresses of blue. They had gathered flowers and rushed up to give them to Billy and others with him. Each visitor found himself walking along holding three or four girls by the hand. They were chattering like little magpies.

It was the same with the little boys dressed in red. There wasn't a shy bone in their healthy bodies. All of the children were anxious to show the presents they had received at Christmas. This was February, but the toys were still almost like new. I thought of the broken toys that littered my house the day after Christmas.

"Just look at them," exclaimed Billy. "They have the joy of God on their faces. There seems to be more concentrated happiness here than any place I have ever seen."

It was evident that the children of Dohnavur were getting next to his emotions, as he visualized the lives from which they had been saved.

Billy wrote in his diary:

"I had something very strange and unusual happen to me at Dohnavur. I cannot yet quite explain it, but I know it must have been from God. As I walked around the grounds, I could not keep back the tears—in fact, I could hardly talk. There was a strange warmness that filled my heart to overflowing.

"I went in to see a Miss Waite, who was Miss Carmichael's nurse for so many years. Tomorrow is her eighty-second birthday. As I was talking to her, I broke down and started crying. I had to turn away. Then I said, 'Let's pray.' Just as I started to pray, I started weeping. (He said, "Oh, God, I feel as if we are on holy ground.") I asked John Bolten to pray, and he wept and prayed. I could not even say good-by to Miss Waite. I was so filled with a strange emotion and I could not account for it.

"We walked about the place, seeing the children and young people. Then we had lunch with some of the workers. We went to Miss Carmichael's room. There we saw the print of where her bed had sat for so many years; twenty years she had been an invalid before she died; twenty years her body was wracked with pain.

"All around the bed were pictures of mountains. They said she loved mountains. She had mountains of Switzerland—the Matterhorn especially she liked, because she was always on the mountain top.

"They said she had the faculty of making everyone who came into her presence feel as though he or she was the only person in the world. They said she ran Dohnavur from her bedside, kept complete control of it, and yet had the wonderful ability of delegating authority.

"The entire place loved and almost worshiped her. They said her writings had made friends for them all over the world. They never ask for money, and yet they need from $6,000 to $10,000 a month to keep the family going. God sends it in. They never tell their needs. It is one of the most worthy places of support that I have seen in India."

Before leaving, Billy saw the family prayer room,

one-day old babies and the spotless hospital where the family's health is protected.

Glancing around again at the buildings, he said:

"Just think, all of this was made possible by the simple faith of one woman."

It was the faith of one woman who was an invalid. She had taken God as a partner to help with her family. He never let her down!

• • • • • •

Billy's Diary:

"In village after village great crowds had gathered to put up a roadblock to stop us, and the police would not let us through until I had gotten up and waved to the crowd. One man stuck a whole bunch of bananas in my hands. People gave us lemons and oranges all the way down. Some would wave palm branches at us. Word had traveled down the highway that we were coming.

"In one section we passed a number of Communist parades. They were parading with their flags waving and shouting their slogans and songs. We got out for several of them so that pictures could be taken. We marched along for about three or four hundred yards with one group. I would wave at them and smile, and they would smile back, because of course most of them, even though they were in red shirts, waving the hammer and sickle, did not know what it was all about. We stopped in front of one group in one little village of Communists that had gathered with their flags waving, and they were all giving their shouts and slogans, with their fists clenched in the popular Communist fashion; so we got out, and I told Bishop Jacob, who was accompanying us part way, to interpret for us. So we quieted the crowd down, and I started preaching to them. I told them what Christ meant to me, that He was the only answer to the world's problems, that I had not come to India to talk politics but had come to talk Christ. And as I began to tell about the change that Christ could give in their lives, they began to drop their clenched fists, until only one man standing in the middle was holding his fists up—but he could not look me in the eye any longer. He looked down, the Holy Spirit was convicting him. I am convinced that the average Communist in India doesn't know what it's all about."

● ● ● ● ● ●

Billy's Diary:

"I have found out that the Church of South India already has some missionaries out, and other groups here are contemplating sending missionaries to other Asian countries. The problem is one of training. There are thousands of volunteers ready to go, but they haven't been properly trained; they are not experienced and equipped enough. However, I have met some of the most handsome, dark-skinned young men, completely dedicated to Christ, that I have ever known. It seems to me that they would make top missionaries in Indo-China, Malaya, and other parts of the East. They could also go to Africa and do missionary work, and in my opinion, be far more effective than the white missionary. I believe the Christians of this area are getting a real missionary challenge, and I believe that we are going to hear from these people."

• • • • • •

Billy's Diary:

"We got here to the hotel in Trivandrum, and it is certainly one of the most unique hotels I've ever been in. The room opens right on to the street and there is no door between me and the street. There is just a little curtain and a little swinging door. People come and stare right in the room while you are going to bed or whatever you are doing; and there was not a mosquito netting in my room and I saw about a dozen mosquitoes on the wall, so I asked for one. They put one on quickly. Paul had a little food there for us to eat, and I have only three people now watching me through the swinging door. Perhaps by the time I go to bed and get to sleep it will be down to two, or even one."

• • • • • •

Billy's Diary:

"On the way to Bangalore the plane had to go up to 10,500 feet in order to climb over the mountains and the very dark clouds—and that is nearly my fainting altitude. When we got up to that height in this DC-3 with no air-pressurizing, I got very faint. It was sort of a good feeling; my head was swimming, I hardly knew what was going on around me. After we crossed over the mountains we came down to about 7,000 and I was much better."

• • • • • •

Billy's Diary:

"While at Bangalore, we saw a number of planes sitting on the ground. One of them was a white plane, which is Dag Hammarskjold's plane, and it was a very strange thing that we had seen him get on the plane the same afternoon that we got on in New York and here way out in the heart of India we see his plane sitting on the ground. It's white, painted with the United Nation's Insignia. Also sitting there was a beautiful two-motored plane with guards standing around. It was a unique plane. I'd never seen one quite like it— probably one of the most luxurious and most shining planes I'd ever seen. I asked someone whose it was, and they said it was Mr. Nehru's plane, and I tried to figure out whether it was British or American. And then someone said, "No," it was Russia's gift to Mr. Nehru. And everybody was standing around talking about it. We looked it over, and certainly from that little bit we could see that Russia knows how to build airplanes.

"But I thought of another thing: We give fifty million dollars in economic aid to India and it appears on the third page; Mr. Nehru is given an airplane costing probably a million dollars and it's front-page news and people talk about it everywhere. There is a showmanship in the way the Russians give that puts all of our giving in the shade. I thought: wouldn't it be a wonderful thing if we gave to India perhaps a beautiful new air-conditioned train; or we might give to Mr. Nehru a white air-conditioned Cadillac. This would cause the people of India to talk more than all of our economic aid put together."

BEWARE OF PICKPOCKETS

Billy Graham and the sacred cow bumped into each other often when the evangelist spent several hours walking through the streets of Benares, India's holy city where every Hindu wants to die.

Hindus believe in reincarnation. They are convinced all who are fortunate enough to die in the holy city will go straight to heaven without suffering the penalty of rebirth. People near death make an effort to get to Benares for their final breath.

Each Hindu, and there are untold millions, feels it is his sacred duty to make at least one pilgrimage to Benares and wash away his sins in holy waters of the Ganges.

Billy stood on the river bank and watched as three dead bodies were burned in piles of wood. Families sat nearby and watched. When all the flesh was burned away, it was the duty of the eldest son to take a pole and knock a hole in the skull to release the spirit. Bones and ashes were placed in the river.

As Billy looked, a body floated down the stream and birds picked away at the flesh. Dead bodies are thrown into the river without being burned. A worshiper stood in shallow water and washed his body with the holy water. Nearby a man filled his jar so others at home could have a drink. Health authorities have found no way to combat such unsanitary practices. Hindus believe no harm can come by drinking the sacred water. At sunrise large crowds gather along the banks to wash away their sins. In the evening they come to sing chants and perform ritual dances.

Some of the gods Billy saw people worshiping were represented by phallic symbols. Such gods depict life. Another place of worship was the monkey temple.

Billy walked through narrow twisting streets, bumping into cows. The animals wandered in and out of buildings with more freedom than humans. Flies and other forms of filth haven't gotten around to recognizing gods, however. The air was choked with bad smells.

Natives streamed in and out of one of the temples. Those going in carried flowers and other forms of tribute for the gods. Near the entrance of one temple was a sign which read, "Beware of Pickpockets."

Benares is a city of 600,000, and some one million pilgrims visit each year. Americans may find it difficult to believe that Benares was famous when Babylon was struggling with Ninevah for supremacy, when Athens was growing in strength, and before Rome had become known. Many cities have fallen into decay, but Benares still flourishes.

Curiously enough, Billy had to drive only a few miles to visit the birthplace of Buddhism, a religion with millions of followers in the Far East. It was at Sarnath where Buddha preached his first sermon after his enlightenment in 520 B.C. A large monument has been built on the spot. Millions journeyed to Sarnath in April to the 2500th anniversary celebration.

It seems that in every place on earth, however, there are a few witnesses for Christ. This was true in Benares. The brightest light seen was Alan Neech, forty-two-year-old Englishman who looked twenty-five. He had been laboring for twenty years in what may be the world's hardest mission field. He asked Billy if it would be possible to come and speak for a few minutes in his church.

Billy had to catch a train that evening for Calcutta. But he said, "I will consider it a privilege."

Neech said there were about 600 Christians among Benares' 600,000 people.

The little church was jammed. What a contrast it presented to the darkness of the Hindu temples! The church was clean and so were the people. Children with scrubbed faces sat on the floor down front.

Billy spoke as if speaking to 100,000. His text was John 3:16. He presented Jesus Christ as the light of the world, then gave an invitation for people to accept and follow Jesus. More than fifty got up and walked to the front.

He had presented Christianity in the heart of Hinduism and near the birthplace of Buddhism. The hungry people responded.

After the service he stepped outside the church and remarked, "Christ has lost none of His power." He glanced back again at the little citadel of Christianity. There was no sign that read, "Beware of Pickpockets."

CHANGE ON A TRAIN

It was early morning and the train was rumbling along through the northern part of India between Delhi and Calcutta.

Everyone in the small traveling group had breakfasted on powdered coffee and cold egg sandwiches. Billy topped his off with a banana. He had eaten so many bananas in India that the monkeys were considering boycotting his meetings.

A short time later, John Bolten and I were alone in a compartment. He was shaving and I was sitting nearby, trying to rally my southern energy for the same task.

C. F. Marconi, a transplanted Italian who had spent most of his life in India and was generally regarded as the best movie cameraman in the country, wandered into the compartment for a bull session. Marconi was a genial good-looking man in his late thirties. He had started filming the tour in Bombay and had been with us in all the cities. He was popular with everyone.

Occasionally, it seemed that I caught Marconi listening to the message when he ordinarily would have been shooting film.

The usual small talk was going on inside the compartment when John, who had gone along on the trip to pray and witness, turned from his shaving and addressed our visitor:

"God has been so wonderful to me. And the most wonderful part of all is that He cared enough for me to send His Son, Jesus Christ."

He paused momentarily and glanced out through the train window as he swished this incredible truth around in his heart again.

"Have you ever really thought about what God did, Marconi?" he continued. "Jesus was His Son—the most precious Person in all the world, but He loved you and me enough to send Him to earth. He was the King of Kings and Lord of Lords, but He wasn't born in a palace. He was born in a stable.

"One of the things that has made the deepest impression on me during this trip is the condition of the stables. Our cards at Christmas show such a beautiful scene. Everything is spotlessly clean. I don't believe it was like that when Christ was born. I think the stable was like those here today—filthy, with rats, flies, and vermin of all kinds.

"Christ was born in a place like this. He grew up and walked among men, perfect in every thought and deed. Then one day He went to the cross and suffered a horrible death because of people like you and me. He took our sins upon His shoulders.

"Doesn't the majesty and glory of such a life and death make you want to belong to Christ, Marconi? He wants to forgive your sins and make you live . . . forever."

Marconi sat there in the compartment and thought about what he had heard. The things he had been thinking about in recent days were coming into focus.

He glanced over at me, as if for reassurance that his thoughts were on the right track.

"It seems to me that the final test of anything is whether it will work," I said. "And Christ does what He says He will do.

"I'm a newspaperman and not a preacher. Maybe I can't explain it right, but, like the blind man in the ninth chapter of John, this one thing I know—a little over five years ago I was a drunken newspaper bum. I had just been fired after three years with the Associated Press and was about to lose the job I had with Chattanooga's afternoon daily, *The News-Free Press*.

"My wife and lovely children were on the greased slide to oblivion with me, because I was the driver. People do a lot of joking about drunks, but there's nothing funny about it when you wake up in the morning and every nerve screams out for a drink. And it isn't funny when the bills come rolling in and the money has already gone out the alcoholic window.

"Then one night, because of the faithful prayers of my parents and wife, I went out to do a human interest story on a preacher, Dr. Fred Garland of Roanoke, Va. He told me what God had done in his own life and then he asked if I didn't want to find the same peace. I wanted peace of mind and soul more than anything in the world. He told me how to find it—through repentance of sin and acceptance of Christ in simple childlike faith.

"It wasn't much of an emotional experience. I saw myself as I really was for the first time and asked God to take over my life.

"He did!

"My life began from that moment. There wasn't any great sudden change, except that I had new thoughts, new motives, and was headed in a different direction.

"Christ made me a better newspaperman. For the first time, I could be depended upon. He made it possible for me to go on these trips and tell the world about the ministry of Billy Graham.

"He can make a better cameraman out of you, Marconi."

At this point, John asked if we couldn't have a word of prayer together. After we had prayed, Marconi began to talk with God, softly and hesitatingly but sincerely.

Then John took him into the next compartment to talk with Billy. The Italian came out, a short time later, with his face aglow.

"I have surrendered my life to Christ for the first time," he said, quietly. Tears filled his eyes.

And the train rumbled on through northern India.

• • • • • •

Billy's Diary:

"We went into one temple that had the most awful, obscene drawings and carvings. The priest would show it to us, seemingly with great delight. These carvings showed various methods of obscenity and immorality. This is all in the name of religion. Of course there is great phallic worship here. I think I felt the powers of darkness and heathenism more in Benares than in any city in which I've ever been.

"This is what Hinduism does. In the middle of all of this heathenism we saw a cross. I asked what that was. It was a little mission school. We went inside. I greeted the little children; they had some little garlands there that they put around my neck. The teacher was so thrilled. John Bolten gave her a little money. And there was a little Christian witness right in the heart of it all. What some of these missionaries pay out here for Christ is beyond description!"

• • • • • •

Billy's Diary:

"We went out to Sarnath, the place where Buddha first got his enlightenment. You know, Buddhism started in India; in fact, Buddha never left India. But India never adopted Buddhism. It spread east to Burma, Malaya, China, and other parts of the Far East. But this was where Buddha preached his sermons and received his enlightenment 2500 years ago. We saw Buddha's old monastery that has been dug up by the British. We saw the old relics of Buddha. We saw the great buildings that are being now prepared by the government because in 1956 they celebrate his 2500th anniversary, and they are expecting literally hundreds of thousands if not millions of tourists to come and see it. Buddhists from all over the world will come here to worship, to pray, to meditate, and to think. It was

hard to believe that here was a man that thought that
he had a teaching from God and has influenced so
much of the world."

• • • • • •

Billy's Diary:

"I spoke for about thirty minutes on the subject:
What Is a Christian? I told them that a Christian is a
person in whom Christ dwelt; that you could be born
in a Christian home, reared in a Christian community,
and still not be a Christian; that you must have a vital,
personal experience with Christ by being born again."

• • • • • •

Billy's Diary:

"Many of the little children were diseased, many
of them had big stomachs from malnutrition. My
heart ached as I realized that a little bowl full of rice
to these children meant everything. They did not
have enough to eat. They did not have any doctors to
come and help them when they got sick. They were
not able to buy any medicine, and I thought of my
own children at home and how much they have in
comparison to these children here in India. My heart
has already gone out to them. I wish that there was
something we could do. There seems to be so little. I
remember the words of Jesus when He said that if we
offend even one of these little ones, it would be better
if a millstone had been wrapped around our necks."

Billy's Diary:

"The men of India dress in every conceivable way. You hardly ever see two dressed just alike. Jerry and I were remarking today that the dress of the men is completely different with almost every man. Right in the main part of town many men wear nothing but G-strings, shorts, diapers; or you may see a man walking along like a London gentleman on a Sunday morning."

ROAD TO PEACE

The 400,000,000 people of India will go behind the
Iron Curtain of communism in less than five years.
And other teeming millions of the Far East won't be
far behind.

That is the opinion of a top American official who
lives in India and who has been trained to look for
significant signs.

India will never go Communistic. Historical culture
and the attitude of the people will never permit Communist domination.

That is the opinion of a member of Prime Minister
Nehru's cabinet.

The opinions were given in answer to the direct
question: "Do you think India will go Communist?"

My short tour of India with Billy Graham doesn't
qualify me as a foreign affairs expert, but it doesn't
take an expert to ask a simple question. And it doesn't
take an expert to see glaring facts.

Two different points of view were given many
times as the question was put to government officials,
taxi drivers, statesmen, missionaries, and other people
from all walks of life. But a majority of opinions and
facts leaned heavily toward the unpleasant picture
that Russia is gaining the upper hand in India, where
the population dwarfs that of the United States.

Here are some things that will aid Americans to see the situation:

India's powerful labor unions and many top government posts are in the hands of Communists. Paralyzing violence is turned on and off by lifting the telephone.

One of the greatest strongholds of communism is in universities. There are strong cells on every campus. Strangely enough, in India there are more Communists among students and white collar workers than among the poorer class. This may be because Russia figures she can get the hungry ones anytime and is concentrating on other groups.

Insurance and medicine have been nationalized, and other big business will follow the same path. Assets are being taken away from the man who has worked hard and accumulated something. One Indian with several companies said: "My days are numbered."

Russian popularity is high. Banner-waving youngsters shouting, "Up Red flag, Up Red flag" march up and down the highways. Most of them don't know why they are marching, but have been told by higher-ups that it is the thing to do. There are no marching bands of Christians waving Bibles, or Hindus praising their gods.

Billy Graham was given a good reception everywhere he went, but Americans, as such, are not popular in India. Newspapers are filled with slanted stories praising Russia and casting the United States in a bad light.

The door to missionaries from America is closing.

The ones already on the scene have seen the hand-writing on the wall and are busily training Indian Christians to take over all phases of the leadership and work. A number of missionaries already have been notified to leave the country.

Freedom, as Americans know freedom, doesn't exist in India. A tourist has to register with police at every city he visits. Only authorized persons can send telegrams abroad. These are censored. Women aren't the only people who are followed in India.

Those are just a few of the signs. All of them point down a rough road for world peace.

• • • • • •

Six people were on the plane with Cliff Barrows when he flew from London to join the team in Delhi. One of the passengers introduced himself to Cliff and said he had become a Christian during Billy's Glasgow meeting in 1955. The plane changed crews in Karachi. The pilot who took over had made his decision for Christ at the same meeting.

• • • • • •

"The greatest disappointment about Mr. Graham's visit to India is that he didn't bring George Beverly Shea with him. Mr. Shea is the most beloved religious singer in all of India" . . . remark by Indian church leader . . . Sales of Bibles skyrocketed in southern India after the meetings, according to an official there.

... A cobra came up out of the grating and got between the bags at the Madras airport when Dr. Paul Maddox and Charlie Riggs were about to catch a plane. The porter almost had heart failure when he reached for a bag and almost grabbed the snake, which was later killed inside the airport waiting room. ... Billy's European documentary film was banned in India because it referred to Russia as "Godless and ruthless" and mentioned the Iron Curtain. It's supposed to be a secret.

• • • • • •

Billy's Diary:

"We have a fellow by the name of Marconi traveling with us and another fellow by the name of Paul Clark. Marconi originally came from Italy. He is considered one of India's top cameramen and he is traveling with us everywhere, photographing our travels. We hope to make a documentary film that will show what God has done during these days. I believe God is speaking to Marconi. He is becoming more and more interested in the gospel."

• • • • • •

Billy's Diary:

"One missionary from the Brethren said she had traveled 400 miles to attend the meetings, and said that she and her people had been praying daily for us for more than two years, and she said it was a very

strange thing to her after all these years in India
to see people so strangely burdened to pray for a man
that they had never seen nor heard, and she said it
could only be the Holy Spirit. I have found this everywhere in India. People have been praying for us for
months, and these people know how to pray. There
is a deep spiritual life among the true Christians that
puts us to shame in America."

FLYING COLORS

What was accomplished during Billy Graham's three-week tour of India, a vital nation in the search for world peace?

An estimated 20,000 made decisions to become Christians, and the Christian belief is directly opposed to communism, now a strong force in India.

The Christian church of India, which numbers some 10,000,000 members, was brought together in a unity never before known. All Protestant denominations, under the leadership of Indians, began working together to spread the gospel of Jesus Christ instead of splitting theological hairs.

Nominal Christians, the kind who go to church on Sunday and then forget about God the rest of the week, were revived. Thousands began living for Christ seven days a week by reading their Bibles, spending time in prayer, witnessing, and being faithful in church.

Over half a million people in India listened with rapt attention to Billy. He made friends for America that could never have been gained by political influence and foreign-aid dollars. He left an impact, with sincerity and straight-from-the-shoulder talk, on rice field workers, textile workers, laborers, professional men, politicians, and government officials.

A unique impact was made on newspapermen of India. Like newsmen everywhere, writers of India are hard to impress. Practically every press conference ended in a theological discussion. Men asked questions about the Bible instead of Senator McCarthy.

A writer stated in the newspaper Amrita Bazar Patrika:

"Billy Graham proved in New Delhi that indeed he is a phenomenon. He was addressing blasé capital journalists who had turned out as numerous as in the case of Mr. Khrushchev. A Russian journalist was among them. He was facing an audience proud not only of Hinduism, but also convinced of the superiority of Hinduism in that it is not a missionary religion and does not proselytize. He was facing people convinced that Christian missionaries were outsiders of imperialism in India and that they are still creating trouble in Assam. He was talking to pressmen who by and large were annoyed by the Portuguese slogan that Christianity is in danger if Goa goes to India and yet Billy Graham came out with flying colors through eloquence and fascinating personality, through tact and sincerity.

"The press conference was something of a journalistic experience, speaking highly of interview and interviewers. With a Bible in hand he made tall claims in modest language and talked about the whole world having the breath of God at present and there were no sneers nor jeers. Indeed there were cheers."

Billy's final day in India was spent in Calcutta where he faced a crowd of over 10,000 and recorded 1,000 decisions. It was the largest religious gathering in Calcutta's turbulent history. Billy was introduced by the Most Reverend Abindra Nath Mukerji, Archbishop of India, Pakistan, Burma, and Ceylon. In the Far East his rank is equal to the Archbishop of Canterbury.

The tour of India, which began with violence and frustration, ended with victory and rejoicing. God had heard the pleas of His people.

• • • • • •

Billy's Diary:

"During the invitation it's not quite as quiet here as it is in our invitations at home. Everybody starts talking. There is a murmur all over the crowd as people start talking. I don't know what they are talking about, I don't know why; and then people start standing up. You see, they are squatting on little grass mats during the entire service, and when the invitation is given, everybody stands up, whether you want them to or not, and they start chatting with each other as the people come forward to receive Christ. Of course an invitation is so unusual with them and so different that they probably are talking about the methods that we are using. Nearly all the pastors that I have talked to, though, are very happy about the invitation and think that it is going to help revolutionize the method of evangelism here in this part of India."

• • • • • •

Billy's Diary:

"It's in the schools that the danger of communism lies. It seems that among the poorer people they are always able to make a living, but among the intellectuals, since the British left in 1947, it is difficult for them all to get jobs. Communism has a tremendous appeal to the intellectuals here in India, and the great danger of communism seems to lie within the intellectual class and particularly among the colleges. One of the things that bothers me is the fact that liberalism has crept into these Christian colleges out here until today very few of them are Christian in the true sense of the word. In some colleges, I am told by both missionaries and Indian leaders, communism has a firm foothold and a grip, even controlling the faculty and student body."

• • • • • •

Billy's Diary:

"I don't think I've mentioned the flowers here in India. India is a riot of color. Even the trees have great vines growing on them that give forth every type of bloom. The yards are filled with all types of flowers that I cannot possibly describe. I don't think, also, that I've mentioned that this is the center of the cashew nut business, that about ninety per cent of all cashew nuts in the world are either grown or processed in this area, and practically all the cashew nuts that we eat in America come from here."

Billy's Diary:

"The eight o'clock meeting this morning in Calcutta was held on the Cathedral grounds with approximately a thousand or fifteen hundred ministers and Christian workers in attendance. I did not have very much liberty because I had on a very heavy winter suit and the sun came up and it was very warm. I don't know why I was persuaded to wear that winter suit, but they told me it might be chilly that early in the morning here in Calcutta, but it wasn't. In addition, I had not slept very well and I was very tired. For a month now we have been giving out emotionally, nervously, physically, mentally, and I am beginning to get weary. However, I believe the Lord blessed. I talked for more than an hour and a half, and I believe that some inspiration and challenge was given to the ministers anyway.

"I shook hands with the Metropolitan. The people rushed all around me, trying to get autographs. I signed a few and then just had to throw up my hands and quit. And one man shouted, 'Is that fair to Calcutta?' I looked at him and smiled and said, 'Now, is that a fair question?' He said, 'No, it's not, I apologize,' because I had been doing my best to sign hundreds of autographs. This is the most 'autograph' country in the whole world. I think the British must have taught it to them, because it's worse than Britain."

• • • • •

Billy's Diary:

"A very lovely and beautiful lady came up to me. You could see that she was a woman of means and culture, bubbling over with personality, the Henrietta Mears type. She had a big Bible in her hand, and I wondered what she was doing with the Bible. She said, 'I was converted eighteen months ago, reading your book *Peace with God!*'

"One lady came to me very shyly, though she looked like a titled woman of means, and said that her son had written and said, 'Please go see Billy Graham because I was converted under his preaching at Cambridge.' She didn't know what to think of it all, and probably thought that her son had gone off the beam. She wanted to see what type of a person I was, that could persuade her son to turn religious, at least that's what she told me."

● ● ● ● ● ●

Billy's Diary:

"When I got back to the hotel, it was hard to realize that the India tour was over. I had preached scores of times, held hundreds of personal interviews, traveled thousands of miles, and seen probably more of India than any other man had ever seen in so short a time.

"But we must at the end of the tour give the praise and the glory to God. This has been beyond anything that we could have planned or worked up. The people of India have responded to the message of the cross

of Christ. There had been the great years of sowing
on the part of the missionaries and Indian workers.
Now this was India's time of reaping. We believe
that the message of these meetings has gone to the
length and breadth of India, encouraging Christians
everywhere to believe that God can use the same type
of evangelism that He is using in other parts of the
world.

"I have come to appreciate, love, and respect these
people. I see their problems, which are immense, their
poverty, their religious superstition that keeps them
bound, the terrible and almost terrifying economic
problems, their social problems, their political problems, their illiteracy, and a thousand and one other
things, such as sanitation and medical needs and malnutrition, and yet I've come to love them with a deep,
abiding love. I have come to realize that the government is facing unparalleled problems that America
will probably never understand.

"It may be that this was God's last call to India. I
don't know. But it is difficult to believe that I have had
the great and glorious privilege of being one of God's
voices on one of His great mission fields. I remember
when I was at Wheaton College, I wanted to be a
missionary, and yet somehow it didn't work out, and
now the Lord has allowed me to go and probably do
more for missions than I could ever have done had I
gone as a normal missionary. How marvelous are His
wonders! How glorious His plans when we commit our
lives to Him!"

INCREDIBLE RESPONSE

Filipinos are hoping Billy Graham will repeat General MacArthur's famous phrase, "I shall return."

The evangelist, faced with the only organized opposition on his tour of the Far East, received a rousing reception and scored one of his greatest triumphs during a single rally in Manila. It whetted the appetites of people for more, and Billy, impressed by the biggest Protestant meeting in the history of the Philippines, may return for a major campaign within the next two years.

Response from the crowd of 40,000 to the invitation at the end of the message was the greatest in Billy's phenomenal history. More than 5,000 walked onto the football track to make decisions for Christ. By comparison, when Billy addressed 120,000 at London's Wembley Stadium in 1954, there were 2,500 decisions.

Billy asked the people to get up and take their stands for Christ. They came from all sections of Rizal Memorial Stadium. Thirty minutes later they were still coming in a steady stream and continued right up to the benediction. Ministers and missionaries looked on in amazement. The people making decisions were not the unloved and the unlovely as some have claimed Christians to be. They appeared to be the cream of the crop, and came from all areas of the Philippines.

Also looking on was American Ambassador Homer Ferguson and many leaders of the Filipino government. The Ambassador had met Billy at the airport when he arrived from Bangkok. They entered Manila under a huge horseshoe which read "Welcome Billy Graham."

His arrival intensified a period of great anxiety for the local rally committee. Some said their faith hadn't been very strong. Things had gotten off to a bad start, they said, when the leader of a strong Catholic church body warned his people not to attend the rally and get "confused" in their faith. In all of his rallies around the world this was the first time Billy had ever been publicly denounced by the Catholic church.

In the face of such opposition, there were some predictions that the crowd would total less than 1,000. Members of the planning committee had more faith than that, however. They engaged an auditorium seating 8,000. Their faith became a little stronger, and a few days later they shifted the site to a larger place seating 18,000. Several days before the meeting, leaders climbed up on the mustard seed and decided to go all out with Rizal Stadium's 25,000 capacity.

Their faith wavered a little a few hours before the rally. Some felt the stadium would be half empty, but the crowd began to arrive early and by the time Billy came every seat was taken. People overflowed onto the playing field, covered two-thirds of it, and sat patiently on the grass.

A lighted sign at the back of the platform stated:

"Jesus said I am the way, the truth and the life. No man cometh unto the Father but by me."

The 1,000-voice choir opened with Billy's theme song "Blessed Assurance," and minutes later doubting pastors sat on the platform with bowed heads as the great choir sang "Great is Thy Faithfulness."

Then Billy startled a few in the audience when he said, "The greatest problem faced by Christianity today is church members who profess the name of Christ but do not live like Christians."

Many of the 5,000 who made decisions were church members.

Before leaving Manila the next day Billy was invited to the palace to have breakfast with President Magsaysay.

And the President observed that Manila had never had a meeting quite like that one the night before out at Rizal Stadium.

• • • • • •

Billy's Diary:

"The arrangers of our crusade here have been Ellsworth Culver, Jack Stoll of the Orient Crusades, who work under Dick Hillis in Formosa. I have come to respect these fellows. I think the Orient Crusades have some of the top men in the Far East."

• • • • •

Billy's Diary:

"Thailand is almost entirely Buddhist. They have hundreds of temples in Bangkok, and they are among the world's most beautiful. There are thousands of priests. We saw priests everywhere in their orange robes. Every young man in Thailand has to be a priest for at least three months. He wears a bright orange robe, goes up and down the street, begging for food from people. People come out and hand him food, and in doing so, they earn a certain amount of merit. The Buddhist system is a great deal on the idea of meriting their salvation, by such good works as that.

"Christianity is relatively new in Thailand, and I believe the first missionaries arrived there approximately a hundred years ago. There are now only 20,000 Christians in all of Thailand. It took thirty-one years of mission work to win even one convert."

• • • • • •

Billy's Diary:

"Bob Pierce took us down through the Chinese section of Bangkok, which was brilliantly lighted, and he said, 'This looks just like Old China used to look.' It looked very prosperous to me. Then he took us to an opium den. Now an opium den is a legal thing in Bangkok, though it is going and probably will be outlawed within the next few years. We were taken down a very busy back alley and then up several flights of stairs and then into this opium den. There, in about fifteen

rooms, lay men in loin cloths. They were smoking
opium. They were lying there in a complete daze, and
girls were giving them massages. It was something
that I never expected to see. The place was very clean,
I must say—extremely so. It was something like a
combination of a gymnasium and a jail because they
were in these rooms that looked almost like prison
rooms, and yet at the same time it sort of had the
smell of a gymnasium. The people were all very clean,
and everything was very orderly, and they greeted us
with curiosity, and probably some wonderment and
amazement. In each of these sort of rooms a woman
would be fixing the pipe, and then the pipe would be
smoked by the various people. I understand that a
lot of the men actually live there. They work during
the daytime in order to have enough money to give
to the opium den, and then they spend their nights
sleeping on the hard boards there and smoking opium
and living in a sort of a daze or whatever way the
opium makes them feel. I understand that some of
those girls work there for nothing, just so they can
breathe the opium. I also understand that there are
cats that come in, and they cannot drive the cats
away, because once they start smelling the opium they
want to stay there. It must be a terrible addiction. I
was glad to see it, but I was also glad to get out. I
thought it was one of the most terrible things we have
seen; and yet remembered that in the United States
we have our terrible narcotics, we have gangs and
drunkenness, two and a half million chronic alcoholics
—so I could not point an accusing finger at the people

of Bangkok for allowing this thing to go on. In fact, this type of addiction seemed to be far more orderly than the type we have in the United States. In fact, I feel much safer walking down the back alleys of Bangkok, Calcutta, or some of these Eastern cities than I do in the back alleys of New York or Chicago."

BAMBOO CURTAIN

The Far Eastern tour of Billy Graham penetrated the Bamboo Curtain of Communist China.

Billy didn't go behind the curtain, but came as close as the law allowed. He knocked on the front door with a big rally at Hong Kong, fabulous free port located just twenty-eight miles away from the barbed-wire border of Red China.

Penetration was in the form of prayer and printed material. Christians in Communist-held Shanghai sent word that hundreds there were praying the Hong Kong rally might strike a spark that would blaze across China. They also sent word that many copies of Billy's book *Peace with God* were being distributed behind the Bamboo Curtain.

One missionary, who will have to go unnamed, told Billy that a copy of one of his sermons was mailed to the pastor of a church in Shanghai. It just so happened that on the following Sunday the preacher hadn't taken the trouble to prepare a sermon. He walked into the pulpit and read the one written by Billy. Like all Billy's sermons, it ended in an invitation for people to accept Christ. A Russian officer was the first one to get out of his seat and make the decision.

Hundreds of thousands of refugees from Red China have poured into Hong Kong in recent years. Emergency housing has been thrown up for them, but there are about 60,000 people in Hong Kong today who are sleeping on rooftops under the most miserable living conditions. According to the refugees, rooftops are far better than the things they had under the Communists.

Bringing word of rising discontent behind the barbed wire, they said soldiers confiscated practically everything they could grow on the land and paid with worthless receipts. They reported sentiment among the people of Red China was swinging back to Chiang Kai-Shek and that many thousands would revolt behind the lines if he invaded the mainland.

Hong Kong is probably the world's busiest listening post. It is from here that the free world listens to Red China and vice versa. Agents from many countries sit around in hotel lobbies and look like a convention of furniture salesmen. But they aren't talking about chairs.

Some may wonder why Communists left the rich plum of Honk Kong for the free world when it could have been taken with a minimum of effort. It isn't so strange. Hong Kong is far more valuable to Red China as a free city than otherwise. It is through Hong Kong that the millions of dollars in war material flow from Great Britain.

Britain rules Hong Kong, and Red China is tickled pink.

• • • • • •

Billy's Diary:

"We got on a beautiful Philippine airliner "Convair" for Hong Kong. The trip took nearly four hours. When we arrived in Hong Kong, it was completely shrouded in clouds and fog. During the fog, the pilot had invited me to sit with him which I did with a great deal of pleasure and satisfaction. It is always a thrill to sit up with the pilot and to watch him operate during a course of flight. The pilot and co-pilot both were interested in our meetings, one of them had been at the meeting the night before and of course everybody was talking about the meetings. The newspapers had given very prominent display of the meeting the night before, and it was the topic of conversation on the plane and everywhere in the Philippines. When we arrived at Hong Kong, the ceiling was at minimum. The Hong Kong airport is one of the most difficult and dangerous in the world. The pilot laughingly said to me that he would not even have tried to make it had we not been on board, but he knew that a great reception was being planned at the airport down below. When we broke through the clouds, we were only about twenty feet from the tops of a mountainous island. It was quite a hair-raising experience. As we came into the airport we certainly didn't miss the mountains by more than fifty to one hundred feet. I waved at Cliff who was in the back of the plane and later told him that I was really waving 'good-by.' Cliff said that it was the most dangerous landing that he had ever made. The airport cannot take the biggest planes due to the fact that it is completely surrounded by mountains. It is considered the world's most dangerous airport, and one of the pilots of the Northwest Airlines told me that he always breathed a sigh of relief when he took off safely from that airport, or landed safely."

• • • • • •

Billy's Diary:

"Hong Kong, of course, is a city of contrast—it is a city of extremely rich and extremely poor. Hundreds of thousands of refugees have come over from China into Hong Kong and as someone has said, 'Hong Kong perches on the coast of Communist China like a fat canary on the shoulder of a hungry tom cat.' There are over 2,500,000 people here, most of them of course are Chinese speaking every dialect of the mainland. You hear the bray of hawkers, the cries of countless babies, the rickshaws, the little old street restaurants, the Chinese riding—but everywhere you are also reminded that this is a British Crown Colony. There is the crisp gesture of the traffic cop and they remind one that here, as nowhere else in Asia, is British law and order. There are the street stalls, the numberless shops which vend glowing jade, laces, carved woods and ivories from the China mainland only a mile away, roasted whole pigs, tin bath tubs, hollow tree coffins, ancient curios compounded of dried sea horses, centipedes, lizards, and snakes. There are over 1500 workshops and factories making everything from flashlights to rubber shoes. The colony consists of 391 square miles and is leased from China until 1997. What happens after that nobody knows."

• • • • • •

John Bolten and I rickshawed up to the South China football field, thirty minutes late for Billy's Hong Kong rally. Over 17,000 were inside. Police had locked the gates. When we posed as members of the team, an officer said: "There are 20,000 people down here in a nearby field who couldn't get in, either. Go down and start a song service for them." And both of us have trouble getting to sing in the congregation back home.

• • • • • •

Paul Maddox told Charlie Riggs he almost talked his way through a British checkpoint near Hong Kong with a Texaco credit card. Replied Charlie, "You could have gone to Peking if the card had been good Gulf."

• • • • • •

Billy's Diary:

"Toward the end of our three-hour journey (from Hong Kong to Taipei) the pilot came back and we had quite a talk. The navigator had once caddied for me on a golf course in Minneapolis, so they invited me up to sit in the cockpit while they came in. It was quite an interesting experience because they had to come through a very heavy overcast down into the Taipei, Formosa airport, and the young co-pilot was just learning to fly out here in the Far East. He didn't look like he had had much experience—he was very nervous, perspiration flowing down his face, because it was his job to bring the plane in. The older man with much more experience had a tough time keeping his hands off the instruments, and it was very interesting to watch them. We came in low over the mountains and landed to a tremendous and tumultuous reception."

DINNER DISCUSSION

"We have tried everything the devil has to offer and found they don't hold water."

The metaphors may be a little mixed up, but the woman doing the talking didn't seem to be. She was Madame Chiang Kai-shek, one of the world's most talented and beautiful women.

The setting was ideal for polite chit-chat, but the chit-chat turned into a theological discussion. Sitting across the table from Madame Chiang at the presidential palace was her husband, the Generalissimo, once ruler of the biggest nation on earth. He lost some of his world popularity when he committed the "great sin" of being opposed to communism. U. S. Ambassador Karl L. Rankin was at one end of the table and his wife at the other. On either side of Madame Chiang were Billy Graham and Cliff Barrows, his music director. A few other guests were present, including Dr. Jim Graham, founder of a Christian college in Formosa, and Dr. Robert Pierce, head of World Vision, Inc.

Chinese food was being served and for a few minutes there was a hum of conversation among the guests. Then Madame Chiang began asking questions. Most of her questions were directed at Billy Graham. The hum faded as everyone strained to hear the conversation between two of the world's most famous people.

One of the first things she asked was "Are people saved who make a decision for Christ and then backslide?" Billy answered, "If the decision was genuine I believe the Bible teaches they are saved, but if a person has sincerely received Christ into his heart, he isn't going to stay a backslider long. He will be so miserable that he will ask God's forgiveness and resume living like a Christian. Some people who think confessing Christ gives them a license to sin are just kidding themselves. They have never been saved."

Madame Chiang has stated she was an intellectual Christian for many years. She believed in God with her head but not her heart. It was only in recent years, she said, that she experienced Christ in a real way and began to grow.

The Generalissimo took little part in the conversation. He doesn't speak English. His face brightened occasionally when Dr. Jim Graham, a gifted linguist, or his wife would interpret a choice bit. Only an outstanding diplomat could have sat there looking pleasant while listening to words he couldn't understand.

The next question Madame Chiang asked was this: "What about people who have never heard of Christ? When they die will they go to hell?"

One person at the table replied immediately: "They are lost." Madame Chiang countered, "I don't believe that." Billy said:

"I don't believe any man can set himself up as a judge and say whether these people are lost or saved. I think that rests in the providence of Almighty God, a God who is holy, pure and righteous. I do believe that the Spirit of God deals directly with some people who have never heard His message. Jungle savages have been found worshiping Christ who have never seen a Bible or listened to a preacher. But our command is to go into all the world and preach the gospel. We should never slacken in our zeal to send missionaries."

One couldn't help but marvel at the nature of the conversation around the dinner table of Nationalist China's number one family. All of the talk was about God, the Bible, and Jesus Christ.

After the guests left the table and retired to the drawing room the Generalissimo answered a few questions through an interpreter. A faithful reader of the Bible, he said his favorite passage was the Twenty-third Psalm. He said also that it was his dream to lead his people back to the mainland of China.

In reply to the question as to what would be his number one prayer request to the Christians of the world, he said he would ask that people be willing not only to pray about stopping communism but to do something about it when they have finished praying.

• • • • • •

Billy's Diary:

"In the helicopter we flew quite low and we could see the villages down below us where the people were getting up, going about their morning chores. The dirt, the filth, and the squalor is almost unbelievable.

"In about thirty minutes we were at the front to

the Seventh Division. The commanding officer met us and we were taken over to a bowl-shaped arena right behind the front lines where several thousand men had gathered for the morning service—sitting out in the open cold. This was the exact bowl I had spoken in three years ago behind the front lines. It was then called Bulldozer Bowl, and now it had a new name. The service was all arranged. Cliff led in a couple of songs and I preached. After the service I gave the invitation for those who wanted to receive Christ and I would say that at least 500 to 1,000 hands were lifted indicating they wanted to receive Christ."

• • • • • •

Billy's Diary:

"In the evening we went to the home of Generalissimo and Madame Chiang Kai-shek. This of course was one of the outstanding events of our entire tour.

"I had met the Generalissimo on my previous trip but had never met Madame Chiang, and I was anxiously looking forward to meeting her. I had heard so much about her faith in Christ. Jim Graham and his wife were invited. So were Ambassador and Mrs. Rankin, American Ambassador to Taiwan, and Mr. and Mrs. Ed Currie (missionary friends). I think Aunt Gay had bought a new dress just for the occasion. They had come over from their station. What wonderful people they are. I fell in love with the Curries all over again.

"We arrived just on time. All of us were gathered in a very luxurious and yet home-like living room, and there we waited for Generalissimo and Madame Chiang to come down. They came in. She grabbed my hand and said how delighted she was to have me; and the General, of course, remembering the past visit, was very enthusiastic in his greeting. He immediately asked me to sit down and asked Jim Graham to interpret. We exchanged greetings, and he was smiling the entire time. I seemed to sense that the light of Christ was in his face.

"Then we went into the dining room and had such a meal as I have seldom seen. I don't know how many courses there were, but it went on and on. And do you know what the conversation was? The very first question after a few greetings had been exchanged was when Madame Chiang said: 'Now if a person sins after he is saved, is he lost or not?' And then we went into a discussion of eternal security that lasted most of the meal. And then Jim Graham got into it and preached a regular sermon. He was talking in Chinese half the time and English half the time; and every time he would start talking Chinese, the Generalissimo's eyes would light up and he would look over. You could tell that he was very fond of Jim Graham, because Jim Graham's Chinese apparently is as fine as can be spoken. I have come to appreciate the great work that Jim Graham has done here, particularly among the top people. Dick Hillis and his wife were at the table with us. Dick has done all the arranging for our Formosan trip and has done a splendid and meticulous job. He hasn't left a stone unturned to make our arrangements the very best possible.

"Madame Chiang and I engaged in some private conversation because I was sitting at her right, and next to me was Ed Currie. She was absolutely charming. I am told that she is something like sixty years of age, but you would never think she was over forty. Her English is absolutely perfect, with more of a New York accent; and her love for Christ and knowledge of the Bible is stupendous. Certainly these are two people who have suffered a great deal in the last few years. They have suffered humiliation. They have suffered betrayal. They have suffered at the hands of their own friends and kinsmen; and yet they come out gloriously triumphant. The Madame said to me that for a long time now she has ceased to think of earthly things. She said, 'My mind is entirely on spiritual things and my eyes are on Christ.' I doubt if there are two statesmen in the world today that are more dedicated to Christ and His cause than Generalissimo Chiang Kai-shek and his wife. I admire their courage.

"Dick Hillis had told me that they like to go to bed early and for us not to stay long after dinner, but it was proper for me as the head of the party to say when. We had been sitting out in the living room for about ten minutes discussing spiritual things when the Generalissimo pulled a black nightcap from his pocket and put it over his head—I think to keep him from catching cold; but I took it as a signal and I got a wink from Dick and we excused ourselves. They had a photographer there taking pictures all the while, so we posed for a few pictures and then we went home."

• • • • • •

Billy's Diary:

"Here in Taiwan there are probably more Christians per capita than almost any spot in the Orient at the moment. Churches are booming, hundreds are being converted to Christ, thousands are studying the Bible, and the door is wide open to the work of the Lord."

A THANKFUL LEPER

People who feel sorry for themselves should visit a leprosarium.

It was a strange congregation that gathered in the little chapel on the grounds near Taipei, Formosa, to hear Billy Graham preach. There were some with no arms, some with no legs. Others had various disfigurements caused by the deadly disease. Probably the greatest pain caused by leprosy, however, is the thoughts and fears of people who don't have it. They shun the leper.

The people sitting in the chapel, by worldly standards, should have been the most miserable on earth. But that was far from the case. There was a strange joy and happiness among the people. They had smiles on their drawn faces.

Cliff Barrows led them in a song. He didn't have to urge them to sing out, as song directors often have to do in American churches. They sang with gusto that was exhilarating.

Sitting down on the front row were four children, two boys and two girls, ranging in age from three to ten. Their faces were marred by the deadly disease that was creeping over their little bodies, but they were singing with all their hearts . . . "Oh How I Love Jesus." They had just never been told they were sup-

posed to feel sorry for themselves. They had a song to
sing and hope in their hearts.

One of the greatest sources of satisfaction to the
lepers, I was told, was that the colony owned one
casket. Before its purchase, they had no way to have
a Christian funeral. Now the casket is used in every
death among the lepers. After the service the body is
taken out, buried, and the casket is put away for the
next to die. And death comes often in a leper colony.

It doesn't take as much to make some people happy
as it does others!

One deformed man, past middle age, said something
rather surprising. He said that he had been a prosperous farmer—all wrapped up in his crops, making
money, and various other things. "I didn't have time
for God in my life. Then I became a leper and with
my separation from all the things I had known I had
time to think about eternal values. I accepted Christ
and found joy. Thank God I became a leper. It was
worth it to find God."

• • • • • •

Billy's Diary:

"In the afternoon at four o'clock we had a tea. This
tea was at the home of General and Mrs. Smyth. He is
the Commander of all the American contingent of
forces in this area. The General and his wife are wonderful born-again Christians. She is one of the most
thrilling and exciting Christians that I've met. Her en-

thusiasm for Christ knows no bounds and the work that she and Sarah Graham have done among the top American personnel and Chinese personnel is one of the most thrilling things that I've seen on my entire trip. There were three colonels that shook hands with me and told me they had been won to Christ by Jim Graham. Then of course we had several generals of the Chinese Army, a number of outstanding leaders among the women of China were there, and all of them were radiant, born-again Christians."

• • • • • •

Billy's Diary:

"The Army sent a helicopter to Taiwan Christian College for me. A great crowd had gathered around, and Captain Bywaters was there to take me. After some juggling, we took off. The wind was so strong against us that we could only make about forty or fifty miles an hour, so it took us about forty-five minutes to get into the Taipei airport, a run that normally should have taken us about fifteen or twenty minutes. It was interesting, though, to watch the reactions of the people down below as they saw the helicopter go over. Chickens and ducks would scatter in every direction. Captain Bywaters said that an airplane will not scare chickens and ducks, but that a helicopter sends them wild. I am sure that some of those farmers are still looking for their chickens."

A SERGEANT'S DECISION

The American Army sergeant in Tokyo sat between his two little daughters as he listened to the message that had captivated audiences in India, Thailand, China, Formosa, and Japan. All around were his buddies in the Far Eastern Command. The speaker was Billy Graham.

The sergeant listened as if he had never before heard the Bible message. It may well have been the first time he had ever heard it in a language he could understand. It was told in a hard-hitting language that pulled no punches.

When the invitation was given, he was one of those who decided that life had something more to offer than he had been getting out of it. He stood with hundreds of others to make a decision for Jesus Christ. Among these was Britain's top general in Japan.

Moments after making the decision, the sergeant reached out with brawny arms and hugged his daughters close to his chest. It was a wordless gesture, but it told a big story.

In Tokyo, Billy was speaking to an American audience for the first time in many weeks. He glanced sideways occasionally as if looking for an interpreter, then warmed to the newly found freedom of speech. In an address to the servicemen, sprinkled with top brass from the Army, Navy, and Air Force, he discussed "Chaos, Cause, and Cure."

He said: "Terror bombs and incredible guided missiles have carried our world to the brink of destruction. The fellowship of fear is universal. Sir Winston Churchill has said we are living in a world balanced by terror. In my talks with President Eisenhower, Churchill, Queen Elizabeth, and other leaders they have not offered any ultimate hope that we can solve our problems. Economic pressures around the world are exploding North Africa in flames. There are racial flareups everywhere. This problem isn't confined to the southern part of the United States. The noose is tightening. History offers us little hope. In 3,000 years we have had 286 years of peace. There isn't time for the next generation to solve the problems. They must be solved in this generation or we will perish.

"What is the cause of all this chaos? It isn't social, political, or economic. We have hatred, lying, bitterness, and intolerance in all cultures and all classes of society and world problems are only reflections of individual problems. Such individuals form nations of hate and nations fight wars. The cause of our problems is the human soul which has a disease—a disease called sin. It's an ugly word, but that's what the Bible calls it.

"What's the cure? We have tried every solution offered by the world and they have miserably failed. We have tried everything but the solution offered by Jesus Christ. The world is too cynical and proud to accept the truth of Christ, but the world will accept it or perish.

"The most astounding thing in all the universe happened some two thousand years ago. God decided to become a man. That man was Jesus Christ. He went to the cross and died in order to do something about the disease of the soul. The cross is the symbol of Christianity. The cross of Christ offers the only solution to personal and world problems. God said He would make you a new person if you would repent, receive Christ, and obey Him. It isn't easy to do. But those are the conditions. It isn't a life for sissies. It takes a man. Will you do it?"

The rough sergeant signified that he wanted to become a man as he hugged his two contributions to the next generation.

• • • • • •

Billy's Diary:

"After going through some very heavy weather, with a lot of winds and bumps in the air, we landed at Okinawa. We had to close the curtains on the plane coming down so you wouldn't see the military. I thought to myself, I've seen pictures of it in *Life* magazine several times, so I didn't need to look out the window. I forgot myself as the plane was coming in, though, and I did peek out, and the stewardess came up and tapped me on the shoulder and said, 'Mr. Graham, please do not look out the window.' So I did not look anymore."

TWO METHODS

General MacArthur conquered Tokyo before he got there, but Billy Graham had to wait until after he arrived.

Different methods were employed. MacArthur used bullets and Billy used a Bible. History will record which of the two methods produced lasting results.

Every major meeting held by Billy set records for the Protestant history of Japan. Residents said few men had so gripped the imaginations of the Japanese people.

Here is a typical example of one day. After addressing the largest group of pastors ever to gather in Japan, Billy called on Prime Minister Hatoyama at noon.

The Japanese Diet, similar to the U. S. Congress, delayed the customary opening thirty minutes to make the visit possible. Billy told the Prime Minister how Christ had changed his life at age sixteen. Then he outlined the Bible formula for world and individual peace.

Hatoyama, who suffers paralysis of the legs and uses a cane like the late President Roosevelt, said he became a Christian as a young man. He added, "Burdens and cares of my office are so great that I couldn't stand up under them unless I could go home at night and turn them over to God."

Hatoyama loves church hymns and is the only

Prime Minister of Japan ever to have one sung at a session of Diet. He relaxes each night at home by listening to hymns. When one of Hatoyama's staff asked if Billy would pray at the conference, the Prime Minister apologized for the fact that he could not stand for the prayer. Billy prayed for him, for Japan, for Russia, for America, and for all nations of the world. His secretary, Matsumoto, said it was the first time he had ever seen Hatoyama shed tears.

Billy had a hard time attending the evening rally at Kokusai Stadium. He couldn't get in because of the crowd. A cordon of police, making use of a half-track, finally cleared the way. The indoor stadium, seating 15,000, was overflowing with 18,000. The crowd outside in frigid weather sent up a clamor saying they would go home if Billy would come out and talk with them. He went out onto the roof and spoke briefly. But few left. They continued the cold vigil and listened to an outside loudspeaker.

In the middle of the address the crowd broke through police lines and several thousand surged into the building. Committee members trembled, fearing that the confusion would break up the meeting. The doors near the platform were crashed open again just as Billy was about to give the invitation. People poured in, but the attention of the listeners was held. There had to be an unseen force at work because most of the police were huddled in a room burning trash trying to keep warm.

Over 1,000 decisions were made. Asked afterwards what he thought about all of the pandemonium back of the platform, Billy replied, "It was one of the most attentive audiences I have ever seen."

• • • • • •

Billy's Diary:

"Japan does not need our educators. Japan has today the highest literacy in the world. The Japanese are the most educated people in the world. There are scores of areas in the United States that need teachers far more than they need them in Japan. Japan does not need our social work. The Japanese economy is one of the most thriving in the world, but Japan does desperately need our message. The message of Christ. She could easily lead the people of the world back to war in the years to come as she did in 1941."

• • • • • •

People in Japan who have colds wear handkerchiefs wrapped around their faces. Looks a little unusual, but makes sense. Saves nose wiping and prevents spread of the cold. It may be an economic instead of a health measure. People can't afford to have colds in a land where preachers make an average of thirty-three dollars a month. . . . The American Army in Japan had a huge Bible and cross carved out of ice at a luncheon in Billy's honor. . . . A top-ranking British general in Tokyo signed a decision card at a Sunday morning meeting. . . . Billy and his interpreter looked like Mutt and Jeff—Billy, 6 ft. 2 in., interpreter, 5 ft. . . . Sgt.

Jacob DeShazer, who made the Doolittle raid on Japan and then returned as a missionary, guided Captain Mitsuo Fuchida into making a decision for Christ. Fuchida was leader of the Japanese squadron which bombed Pearl Harbor.

• • • • • •

Billy's Diary:

"How Tokyo has changed. I could notice it on the way in. The traffic, the thousands of neon lights, the people were better dressed, and there is something about this country that reminds me of Germany—its strength, its power, the hard-working people—they are industrious."

• • • • • •

Billy's Diary:

"In talking to the Japanese so far, it seems to me that they have a great deal more independence, more courage to stand up and talk to you since they have received their complete independence. They are very kind and courteous and gracious, but they meet us now more on the level of equals rather than almost servants as it was three years ago when I was here, and they were still an occupied country. This of course is natural and as it should be."

BRIEF MINISTRY

Billy Graham intended to talk on evangelism but never got around to it.

About 1,200 missionaries from every city and village in southern Japan were gathered at Osaka to hear the young preacher most of them had prayed for but few had seen. A large majority of the missionaries were from America.

Billy announced his text and then started talking about something else. It was very informal. He was among home folk who loved God enough to leave their loved ones for Him.

He said:

"Bless your hearts. You should be preaching to me. Your devotion and sacrifices have been far greater than mine." He told them about great crowds that came to hear the gospel of Christ in Great Britain, Europe, and India.

And then he said:

"I want to tell you something that I haven't told others on this trip around the world. I feel tonight as if my ministry is going to be very brief. My name has appeared in too many newspapers. It has been placed on too many posters. There has been too much praise given to a man and the Bible says God will not share His glory with any man."

He added:

"If there are any newspapers in heaven, the name
of Billy Graham will not be on the front page. Head-
lines will be about some unknown missionary back in
the jungles who has been faithful."

After telling about the big crowds attending the
meetings, he discussed some of the reasons for his unusual ministry. He said: "The number one thing has
been prayer. People around the world have prayed.
God answers prayer. The great need on the mission
field today is not a new method or more money, even
though we don't give enough. The big need is more
prayer from folks at home. They should join you in
saturating the work with prayer.

"The second reason for our success has been the
power of the Holy Spirit. A human being can take
another just so far toward heaven. God's Spirit must
do the rest. All of us need to be filled with the Holy
Spirit. There were only 120 people at Pentecost, but
they went out and shook the world in one generation.
We have more of everything than they had, except
one. They were filled with the Holy Spirit.

"The message is important—not the messenger. The
trouble with many preachers today is that they are too
proud to preach the simple gospel that people can
understand. I used to be too proud myself. I have found
that I cannot win anybody for Christ unless I preach
about the cross on which He died. There is a power
in the cross that is found in no other place in the Bible.
And I have found that I must preach the resurrection.
Christ didn't stay in the grave. He rose again. I worship a triumphant, living Christ. Some of us Christians

go around with long faces as if we are attending a funeral.

"Another thing that revolutionized my ministry was the day I accepted the Bible as God's inspired Word. Back in 1946, '47, and '48 I had doubts about some parts of the Bible. And when I preached, I had no power. I fell on my knees and told God I was going to get out of the ministry unless I found a message with power. From that day I have accepted the Bible as God's inspired Word to man and have preached it with authority.

"These are unusual days. The Spirit of God is moving across the nations of the world in a way never seen before. It is easier to talk with people about Jesus Christ today than any time in living memory. I wouldn't trade places with the Apostle Paul or any of the others who lived in the past. This is God's hour for the church. Let's be faithful to the task God has called us to do."

He seemed to be a different Billy Graham as he talked with the missionaries.

Maybe they can hear the address on evangelism on his next trip around the world. . . . unless his ministry is cut short.

● ● ● ● ● ●

Billy's Diary:

"On the outside (of the meeting in Osaka) I could see many missionaries that had come from a long way. I was very sorry that they were unable to get in. During the service on the inside of the building that was supposed to hold 3,000, but probably had about 6,000 jammed in it, they were sitting in the windows, hanging up on the rafters, etc. It was quite a dangerous looking sight to me. There was no possibility of course, of giving an invitation to get people forward, because no one could move. I preached—Mr. Saki did my translation for me. What a meeting! I was so tired I could hardly stand on my feet. I had to shake my head several times during the sermon to keep from blacking out. This was the first time on this trip that I've really been so weary that I could just not stand on my feet."

SINGING AT MIDNIGHT

The first reaction to pock-marked Korea is, "What did they ever find to fight about over here?"

That is the second reaction, too.

The land is mountainous, desolate, bare and yields a meager living to the people. For sheer ruggedness, the Korean fight must have been one of the worst of all times.

Weather also goes to the extremes. The typical winter day, with howling winds that cut to the bone, would make a December day in America seem like May, in comparison. Torrid summers are just as bad in the other direction.

On the morning after Billy Graham's meeting in Seoul, people were freezing to death on the main streets of the city. Dr. Bob Pierce came upon the body of one man as he walked along a street. The fellow had been covered by a straw mat until he could be taken off for burial.

It is the inhabitants of Korea that touch the heart. The land is poor, but the people are wonderful. They are worth fighting over. They have simple faith, humility, and friendliness that go deep into the heart and affection of others.

Members of the churches have a prayer meeting every morning before daylight, often in churches without walls. Wintry winds just don't seem to make a difference.

The Christian church of Korea probably has suffered more than any in history. Thousands of ministers have been killed by the Communist armies and even more thousands of Christians have been put to death. But the Korean church today is one of the healthiest on earth—growing in strength daily without the many divisions evident here. The Korean church is paying its own way and sending missionaries out to the field.

The people live in one of the most desolate countries to be found. Poverty is everywhere. Disease cuts a wide swath. As the world looks at things, the Koreans have very little to be happy about.

But, like Paul and Silas, beaten and in chains, they are singing at midnight.

• • • • • •

Billy's Diary:

"You can't help but admire Syngman Rhee. He's a great stalwart giant. He's every inch a Christian, a Methodist, a man with very strong ideas about the world in which we live. He's very dogmatic in his desire to get Korea united at any cost. You can understand something of his feeling and when you talk to him you sympathize with his position. He is the George Washington of Korea. Suppose George Washington had said, "No, let's try to gain our independence from Britain by peaceful means." We might never have had the American independence as we have today. Syngman Rhee is somewhat the same way. He is ready to go to war if necessary to reunite his country. He sees the industry in the North, the agriculture in the South. He knows that his little country cannot exist being divided the way she is; he is very bitter against communism and the Japanese. He's fought communism and the Japanese all his life and at the age of seventy-eight, he's ready to fight again."

• • • • • •

Billy's Diary:

"We were taken by the military police out to a little orphanage that Bob Pierce had just paid for out of World Vision and had a dedication service.

"It's a beautiful orphanage out on the hillside. I think it is to be operated by the Presbyterians and they had the nurses and doctors ready to help. These were children that were orphans by American soldiers. There are thousands of children all through Korea that were left by American soldiers of Korean mothers. The American government has tried to take some responsibility towards these. It's a very difficult situation. The chaplain says that hardly a week goes by but what some baby is left at the chaplain's office by a mother with a note saying, "If you don't want it kill it. I can no longer support it."

• • • • • •

An observer said that during World War II the Japanese wouldn't admit that Formosa had mountain peaks higher than 12,425-foot Mount Fujiyama. Actually, he said, there were two higher peaks in Formosa, but Nippon maps showed them to be a few feet lower. After the end of the conflict a planeload of Japanese bigshots were flying to Taipei. The pilot checked his map and found he was high enough to clear the peaks. Then bang—everyone was killed.

• • • • • •

Billy's Diary:

"The press had gathered in force. They asked questions for an hour and a half.

"There were not only questions about world conditions and communism, but there were questions on theological matters. It's very strange that almost everywhere we have been, the press conferences have been theological conferences. These people really want to know what Christianity teaches. I am afraid that some of our preachers have not come right out and told them straight out in blunt, plain words what Christ really means, and so I tried to say straight out what Christianity is, and I have found great respect for the message everywhere."

• • • • • •

Billy's Diary:

"The taxi driver that drove us over to the meeting tonight scared us to death. He would drive about sixty down a street and slam on his brakes and we would practically sit up in the front seat. We were getting so nervous that I asked Don Hoke (a missionary) to ask him if he was a tank driver during the war. He asked him, and he said, sure enough, he was. That was his job during the war—to drive a tank. I finally covered my eyes with my hands so I wouldn't have to see what all was going on. Charlie Riggs was sitting there, and he said that he counted five times where we almost had a fatal crash. These taxi drivers in Tokyo would put our New York taxi drivers to shame."

• • • • • •

Billy's Diary:

"We were taken to the Throne Room of the Emperor. The Diet Building is a very beautiful building, built entirely of Japanese material, and they are very proud of it. One fourth of the entire cost of the building went into this one room where the Emperor comes twice a year to open the Diet. The chandeliers, the silk carpets, make it probably one of the most fabulous rooms anywhere in the world. The Emperor also has a private entrance with maroon carpeting that in itself is quite majestic."

PEACE IN KOREA

The U. S. military provided Billy Graham with a plush C-54 and not so plush helicopter for his two-day trip to Korea, but he was not on a junket. Every time he looked up he was speaking to thousands of people.

He looked up once and was near the thirty-eighth parallel, now a No Man's land with alert Americans and Communists on both sides. Some of them are trigger happy under the uneasy truce—not peace. On the day before Billy's arrival UN forces fired 1,000 rounds of ammunition.

During his busy morning at the front, Billy spoke to thousands of American soldiers from the Seventh and Twenty-fourth divisions. Some of them rode over two hours in open trucks during freezing weather to hear the preacher from back home. Several hundred raised hands as an indication they believed what he said.

The largest crowd to hear the evangelist was 60,000 on Sunday afternoon in Seoul. Among those in attendance was President Syngman Rhee, an old war dog who thinks that Americans are pretty stupid for not resisting communism with force. He wants to storm back across the parallel and unify Korea come what may.

On the night before the afternoon rally, a missionary and I were walking along a frozen road and he said, "If it stays this warm there's no telling how many people will turn out for the meeting tomorrow." I glanced over at him to see if he was trying to pull my numb leg, which was in the first stages of frostbite. He was serious. It turned out that the weather was very warm for Korea, but there wouldn't have been fifty Americans out for the Sunday service.

The people who sat patiently and listened as the chill wind whipped across the stadium were the same people seen in newsreels as they trudged up and down Korean roads as refugees escaping from the Communist armies. Little children had lost their scared looks and romped around the edges of the crowd.

There were some children, however, who were not present. Their parents were ashamed of them and kept them hidden in back rooms. The reason for their shame was that the children were half-castes left behind by their UN fathers. The most despised persons in Korea are half-castes. The little boys and girls, even though they had nothing to do with their pitiful plight, face lives of suffering as outcasts. Some of them have been secretly killed by Koreans and none will ever be accepted by society. Missionaries, with Bob Pierce's World Vision leading the way, have rescued a few of the children and are endeavoring to find them Christian American homes denied by indifferent fathers who had gone out for a night on the town.

Cliff Barrows, music director for the Graham team, had been supporting one—a six-year-old Korean boy— with monthly contributions, but he had never seen him until the visit to Seoul. The boy, named Kim, was brought to him at the orphanage. Cliff picked him up and hugged him tight. It must have been the first time anyone had ever shown Kim that he was loved and wanted. He grabbed Cliff around the neck and wouldn't let go for thirty minutes. The most awful thing in the world is not to be wanted.

Cliff conducted his part of the program with the little fellow in his arms. Finally he had to leave in order to catch the plane back to Tokyo. There were tears in the eyes of the big American and the little Korean. They had never seen each other before, but love had covered the gap in a matter of minutes.

● ● ● ● ● ●

Billy's Diary:

"It was as if seven devils were in the crowd stirring them up with pitchforks. I never have held a meeting quite like it. One of the things I think they did wrong was that they put 5,000 children right down in front and these little children sitting on the cold ground had been sitting for two hours before the service started and you know how children are! They don't like to sit that long and they were getting up and moving around and some had to go to the bathroom—I felt as though we could never get the service going."

● ● ● ● ● ●

Billy's Diary:

"The men crowding around afterwards seemed very hungry to talk about home. These men live a very difficult life. Sixteen months they have to stay in Korea when they come, and that's sixteen long, hard months. They have very little entertainment, very little recreation. The villages are off limits to them and the generals have to keep them busy in military activities, physical recreation. They do have some bowling alleys and films are shown and chapel services conducted, but that is about all, and these men lead a very rugged life, because there's no fighting and most of them do not realize why they have to be there. It's very strange that 10,000 miles away from home they have to be manning lines in a country that is almost forgotten at home. And so I felt that the men were a bit discouraged with their lives. They crowded around for autographs, pictures, and then we were taken back to our helicopter, took off for the next base and in about fifteen or twenty minutes the beautiful Korean terrain could be seen, which this time of year is very bare. And then we landed at the next division.

"The helicopter came down right beside where the men had already gathered and on this occasion the men had to stand. The Swiss and Swedish truce teams were there. There were Turkish soldiers and New Zealand soldiers, British soldiers, American soldiers and I believe they said about eight various nationalities were represented. I spoke there again and several hundred men lifted their hands to receive Christ."

BACK ROOMS OF LIFE

Can you imagine a mother being ashamed of her child?

Can you visualize the hurt look in the face of a little boy or girl who has never been hugged tightly to the breast and is made to feel unwanted in many heart-touching ways?

Can you picture grandparents coming for a visit and, in the usual way of grandparents, making much over some of the children and never speaking to one of them?

I can! There are thousands of tiny boys and girls like this in Korea. They are unwanted, unloved, and unhappy—as only a boy or girl can be unhappy.

They spend most of their time hiding in back rooms. They never play with other children, because the other boys and girls will not have anything to do with them. They never know the joy of getting something new.

They go to bed without a goodnight kiss and they get up in the morning without a friendly word of greeting. And the most heart-rending thing of all is that they don't know why.

What kind of strange children are these, who live such miserable lives? Some may imagine they are horrible and deformed, but that is not the case. They are among the most beautiful children on earth.

The only thing wrong with them is that they are

unfortunate enough to have a Korean mother and an American father, who has long since forgotten about the time he went out for a night on the town. The children are half-castes. And half-castes are despised by Koreans, who think that their race should be of a pure blood.

A little child, of course, knows nothing about the thinking of so-called enlightened adults, with their hates and customs. The only thing the child understands is that he isn't wanted.

Something is being done for hundreds of such children, but thousands more remain in the back rooms of life. Missionaries, led by World Vision, Inc., are starting orphanages in Korea and finding American homes for many of the children.

I walked into the home of a missionary one cold night in February. A three-year-old girl bounced up off the bed and threw her arms around my neck.

She had been made to realize that some people loved her. This little girl was waiting to leave for America, where she will be the daughter of Roy Rogers and Dale Evans. How different her happy life will be on the California ranch from the one she would have suffered in Korea.

One morning we went out to an orphanage near Seoul. Cliff Barrows, a man with one of the world's great hearts, had been supporting a boy named Kim at the orphanage. Every month he sent ten dollars halfway around the world to care for a boy he had never seen. Kim, three, had been told a man in America provided for him, and that he was going to visit the orphanage. They brought Kim out after we arrived. Cliff reached down and picked him up. They looked at each other and then Cliff hugged him tightly.

Who can describe the look of joy in the eyes of a boy as he nestles in the arms of a man and realizes he is loved and wanted?

SENSE OF HUMOR

A sparkling sense of humor seems to be one of the balance wheels that keeps members of the hard-working Billy Graham evangelistic team on an even keel.

They are serious when the occasion calls for seriousness, but when a light word is needed to break the tension, somebody usually comes up with it.

Once, after Billy had delivered a lengthy sermon on the inspiring courage it took for Daniel to enter the lion's den, his aide, Dr. Paul Maddox, chief of chaplains for the European Theater during World War II, said:

"I want to tell you something, Billy, those lions weren't scared either!"

A woman in an audience almost became hysterical with mirth once when the Rev. Grady Wilson, associate evangelist, told about the old southern preacher who began reading his text one Sunday morning, without realizing that some playful boys had glued several pages of his Bible together.

The preacher read:

"When ole Noah was 120 years old, he took unto himself a wife." Then, turning what he thought was one page, he continued:

"She was 140 cubits long and 40 cubits wide, built out of gopher wood and covered with pitch inside and out."

The preacher stopped at this point and said, "Now, brethren, that's the first time I've ever seen that in the Word of God, but if the Bible says it, I believe it." Scratching his head, he said, "That just goes to prove another Scripture passage that says, 'we are most fearfully and wonderfully made.'"

On another occasion Grady told a group about the chicken thief who was converted and joined a church. He said:

"This fellow had made a trade out of stealing chickens. He didn't know how to do anything else. After his conversion he searched the Bible for scriptural authority so he could continue stealing chickens. In the New Testament he found a verse that said: 'Let him that stole, steal no more, but rather let him labor with his hands that which is pleasing unto the Lord.' With a little ingenuity and changes of punctuation, the chicken thief found his authority. He quoted the verse thusly: 'Let him that stole steal, no more let him labor with his hands.'"

At a luncheon in Glasgow last year, Billy was addressing one of the most distinguished groups ever to gather in Scotland. Lords, ladies and earls were a dime a dozen. It was a very serious occasion. Just as he was getting into the heart of the message, a woman fainted.

Lee Fisher, another aide who helps Billy on research, was sitting nearby and felt compelled to go to her aid when none of the Scots made a move. She was a big woman, with many extra pounds of distinction, and Lee had a hard time lifting her from the chair. He glanced frantically around, pleading with his eyes for help. The Scots sat unmoved, concentrating on the speaker. He finally got the portly woman up in his arms to take her out, and almost dropped her before another member of the Graham team came to his rescue.

As soon as the meeting was over Billy found Lee, who seems to have a knack of getting into embarrassing situations, and said:

"Well, Lee, you've done it again. I was doing fine up there. Had all my thoughts under control when I looked up and saw you staggering around with Lady Whatchamaycallit in your arms. I lost track of everything I was going to say."

• • • • • •

Billy, usually one of the most flawless of speakers, has his off moments.

During one sermon, while trying to say, "Hail fellow, well met," he said, "Fail mellow, hell met." In an attempt to straighten it out he made it worse—"Hail mellow, well fet."

On another occasion, he tried to say, "Six of one and a half-dozen of the other," but he said, "Six and a half-dozen of one or another."

• • • • • •

A lady in Texas once protested to Grady Wilson about his use of the words "old maid" in a sermon.

He begged her pardon and promised in the future he would refer to them as "unplucked jewels."

The lady then opened her Bible and showed Grady her bibical reference for never marrying. She had circled in red pencil part of one verse, which read:

"I would not have you ignorant, brethren."

She ignored the comma!

• • • • • •

Penetrating analysis . . .

A man from America wrote Billy Graham that God would not bless the United States because of one significant thing. And that, he said, was the digging of the Panama Canal. To support his serious thought, he quoted from the Bible: "What God has joined together, let no man tear asunder."

THE BIBLE SAYS

Billy Graham's 40,000-mile speaking tour of seven countries in the Far East proved that the heart and soul of man is the same among all races.

The tour showed beyond all question that people react the same way to the message of God even though they may have skins of different color, speak many languages, and live in cultures centuries apart.

Billy preached one message, with little variation, to an estimated 1,000,000 people of India, Thailand, Philippines, China, Formosa, Japan, and Korea. He had been warned there would be little response in most of these countries where dominant religions are Hinduism, Buddhism, and Shintoism. Over 40,000 responded. There seemed to be no difference in reaction to that seen when he preached at Chattanooga, St. Louis, Toronto, London, Paris, or Berlin.

What was the message with such strange powers? What text could produce such results? Readers are likely to be amazed with its simplicity. His text for every major address was John 3:16, the most familiar verse in the Bible: "For God so loved the world, that he gave his only begotten Son, that whosoever believeth in him should not perish, but have everlasting life." Billy explained it in a language a child could understand, but adults were gripped with attention.

Here are the highlights of the sermon just as delivered by Billy:

"All of you know about this verse, but few of you know what it says. It begins with these words 'For God.' Who is God, some of you may ask. I'm going to tell you what the Bible says about Him. God is the one who created the universe. He made the sun, the moon, and the stars. He made you. Now God does not have a body like us. God is a spirit. He is in Russia. He is in Africa. He is in India. He is here tonight. There's something else I want you to understand about God. He is an impartial God. He is no respecter of persons. You can't pull any strings with Him. He loves Russians just as much as He loves Americans. He is holy, pure, and righteous.

"There are some people in the Far East who have the idea that Christianity is a Western religion. That is not true. Christianity was in the East long before it was in the West. Christ was born between the East and the West. His skin was not as light as mine nor was it as dark as some of the people who live in the East. I like to picture Christ as one who can stretch out His arms to the East and West.

"Let's see what else the verse has to say. It says 'For God so loved.' Some may ask, Why was the human race created? Were we created to have all these troubles, frustrations, and fears? No. God created man to love Him. God is a God of love. In order for there to be love there has to be an object to love. God created man and placed him in a paradise. They walked together in the cool of evening. They loved each other.

"But God gave man a great gift. He didn't create him like we do an automobile with push-button control. He gave him freedom of choice. He didn't want man to love Him because he had to do it. He wanted man to love Him by choice. So He gave man a test.

"He told him there was one fruit in the garden that he should not eat. If you do, God said, you shall die. Man ate the fruit. He disobeyed God. He rebelled against God. With that rebellion sin came into the world. Every person since that time has been born in sin. But, you say, wait a minute, Billy, surely you aren't going to say that all of us will be punished because of Adam's sin? That's not all of it. When you reached the age of accountability—an age when you could make decisions for yourself—you became a sinner by choice. You disobeyed God because you wanted to.

"Now you ask, What is sin? I'm going to tell you. You have a body. You have eyes, ears, nose, hands, and feet. One of these days your body is going to die and be placed in the grave. But you're more than a body. You're a living soul. Your soul is your intelligence. It has memory, hopes, and fears. Those are things that are characteristics of the soul. Your soul was created to live forever. It is going to live forever whether you like it or not. I know a man who took a revolver and blew his brains out. He only killed his body—not the soul.

"And there is something wrong with the soul. The soul has a disease. It is worse than cancer or leprosy. The thing that is wrong with the soul has caused all of the troubles and wars we have ever had. It has caused every difficulty in your personal life. Do you want to know what it is? The disease is an ugly word that God called sin.

"All of us are afflicted with it. You're a sinner. I'm a sinner. The Bible says all have sinned and come short of the glory of God. And the Bible says the wages of sin is death—eternal separation from God in a place that Jesus called hell.

"The disease of sin is everywhere. You can go to the headwaters of the Amazon River in South America where savages live. You will find these savages lying, cheating, hating, and filled with lusts. You can go to New York City where there is great culture, with one of the highest standards of living the world has ever known. You will find the people of New York lying, cheating, hating, and filled with lusts just like the savages.

"Your soul was created in the image of Almighty God, but sin has separated your soul from God. He is holy and righteous. Sin cannot stand in His presence. Your soul longs and hungers for God but cannot make contact because of sin.

"Wouldn't it be wonderful if the whole human race could go to a doctor and get an injection that would cure all bitterness and hatred in the world? Wouldn't it be great if such an injection could make us love everybody? The world doesn't offer such a serum but God does. He has provided a way for our sins to be forgiven. He has made it possible for you to have peace and joy instead of misery and pain.

"God loves you. He cares for you. He knows everything about you. Don't ever think this is such a great big world that God doesn't have time for you. He has the hairs of your head counted and He has a name for every hair. He knows where you live. He knows every thought of your head and heart.

"I was walking along one day and accidentally stepped on an ant hill. Many of the ants were killed. Scores were hurt. Their home was wrecked. I felt very sorry for the ants. I wanted to tell them how sorry I was and help them rebuild their home, but I couldn't do it. I was too big and they were too little. We couldn't talk to each other.

"God looked down from heaven one day. He saw all the unhappiness and trouble in the world. He loved us and wanted to help us. But He was too big and we were too little. We couldn't understand. What did God do? He did the most astounding thing ever done. God decided to become a man. That man was Jesus Christ. Jesus Christ is God. He walked among us. He spoke our language. He healed the sick. He made the blind to see, the deaf to hear, and the lame to walk. He was God.

"Christ did something about the sinful condition of man. He went to the cross and died. The cross is a symbol of Christianity. On every Protestant and Catholic church there is a cross. Why? Because it was on the cross that Jesus paid the penalty for sin. He died in your place. They put spikes in His hands and feet. They put a crown of thorns on His head. They spat in His face. But the greatest suffering that Christ did on the cross was in the moment He cried, 'My God, my God, why hast thou forsaken me?' It was in that moment that every sin you have ever committed was laid on Christ. He died and was placed in the grave. But He didn't stay in the grave. In three days He rose again. He is now sitting at the right hand of God the Father in heaven to make intercession for you.

"Christ died in order that your sins could be forgiven. He took the hell that you and I deserved. That's what God did. But you have to do something if you are ever going to heaven. There are three things that you must do. Listen carefully. These are the requirements of God—not Billy Graham.

"The first thing you have to do is repent. The Bible says unless '. . . ye repent, ye shall all likewise perish.' What does repentance mean? Repentance means that you must confess your sin. You must confess you have failed God. That's not easy to do. None of us like to admit we are wrong. None of us like to humble ourselves, but we must do it. That isn't all repentance means. It means that you must renounce your sins. You must be willing to turn your back on them. It doesn't do any good to confess your sins unless you are willing to renounce them. You can't have your sins and Christ at the same time.

"The second thing you have to do is receive Christ. How do you do that? You receive Christ when you invite Him into your heart as Lord and Master and Saviour. You can't understand it all. I don't. You have to trust Him by faith. Faith goes beyond understanding. Faith goes beyond reasoning.

"Suppose I go out to the airport in Manila to catch a plane for Hong Kong. I buy a ticket. The plane is standing there ready to take off. It is a beautiful plane. I have faith in the plane. I believe it can take me to Hong Kong. I have a ticket, but the plane goes down the runway and takes off without me. Why? I failed to do one thing. I failed to get on board. You must take the positive step of getting on board with Christ and believe by faith He will take you to heaven.

"The third thing you have to do is obey Christ. You must live for Christ. I have searched the Bible from cover to cover and no place can I find where it says you can be a Christian and live any kind of life you want to live. How do you obey Christ? You obey Christ by reading your Bible every day. The Bible is food for your soul. It helps you to grow. You obey Christ by spending time in prayer every day. You can pray anywhere—walking down the street, sitting in your home, or driving your car. God will hear your prayers and answer them. You obey Christ by witnessing for Him. How do you witness? You witness, first of all, by the way you live. People will see you are different and begin to ask questions. Then tell them about Christ. Another way you obey Christ is by being faithful in your church. Christ is the head of the church and He has commanded you to worship and serve Him there."

That was the message. It was as simple and profound as that, and people responded to it—a Hindu professor, Buddhist priest, drunkard, European royalty, American millionaire, and street sweeper.

"You don't have to believe it," said Billy. "That's your academic privilege. I have only told you what the Bible has to say."

RUSSIAN OVERTURE

Billy Graham was asked a number of times during his tour of the Far East if he would accept an invitation to speak in Russia.

His answer was "yes"—provided certain conditions are met.

The conditions—complete freedom to preach the gospel of Jesus Christ through his own interpreter.

It is not generally known, but Billy received an invitation last year to speak in Russia. The invitation reportedly was received during the World Baptist Alliance in London, where Billy was the featured speaker.

The invitation stipulated that the meeting would be inside a church—not a giant outside rally that might attract over 100,000 persons—and that it would not be preceded by a publicity build-up. The matter of who would provide the interpreter was discussed, with no definite agreement reported.

Billy wanted to go, but he didn't want to be used as another propaganda weapon in the Red peace offensive. He spent much time in prayer about the invitation. He talked it over with President Eisenhower and Secretary of State Dulles.

Sources close to all three said they were in agreement on accepting the invitation if Russia met the conditions of complete freedom. To date, the visit remains in the talking stage.

The church meeting, with the crowd limited to the capacity of a building, presented the possibility that Russia would have Billy face a stacked house, where there would be no response from the people on orders of the Kremlin. Billy said he was willing to go in the face of this possibility because of his faith that the gospel of Christ is more powerful than the schemes of men.

The Rev. J. I. Zhidkov, president of All Union Council of Evangelical Christian Baptists, said last year that Baptist churches in Russia enjoyed full freedom and were "always full."

This may be true, but such talk is in direct contradiction to Marx' stock answer against Christianity. He said, "Religion is the opiate of the people. Christianity is used by the classes to enslave the masses."

And this opinion of Christianity has not been refuted by the present Russian leaders. He said there may be times when communism will zig and times when it will zag, but that the ultimate aim always will be world revolution—with no place for God in the master plan.

Billy has gone on record with the statement that "individuals and nations which embrace communism are individuals and nations which have rejected God. The heart of man is so designed that it must embrace some kind of religion. If it cannot bring itself to accept the true gospel of Christ, it invariably embraces some

kind of false ideology. Today millions are embracing
the false religion of communism.

"The creed of communism is to divide and over-
throw. It is in direct opposition to the teaching and
spirit of Christianity. It is Satan's philosophy. Jesus
taught not the survival of the fittest, but the revival
of the unfit. Communism does not recognize the personal man for whom Christ died. It is the proletariat
and they must rule at all costs, even if it takes the slay-
ing of half the world to accomplish their purposes."

Billy may never go to Russia, but if he does he will
go with complete freedom to preach about Jesus Christ,
who taught the value of the individual and said:

"For what is a man profited, if he shall gain the
whole world, and lose his own soul? . . ."

• • • • • •

Billy's Diary:

"I have not been sick one single day. I do not have
any cold, sore throat, or stomach ache. Everything
has been absolutely perfect. I do not know where the
strength has come from for the various activities that
we have been called upon to do on this trip. It's really
beyond me. It certainly hasn't been strength that I
normally have. I just don't have this strength. It has
been God's strength daily. I have of course felt a great
tiredness, but there has always been strength for the
task. The Lord also has given me great grace in being
patient, with all the various responsibilties and problems that have presented themselves. In no way do I

say it boastfully, but I say it to His glory. I have not lost my temper once and try to wait patiently on everybody. I have also felt something else that has been very strange, and that is an expectant faith all the time, continually believing that something is going to happen, believing that the strength will be there; and I have been very conscious of God's presence continually.

"We have decided to go home on the *President Cleveland* in order to get a few days' rest before landing in Honolulu."

MOST IMPORTANT THING

Billy was in good health, but he seemed to be physically and mentally exhausted as he turned his eyes homeward after the final service in Korea.

There was another service remaning—in Honolulu —but there was going to be some rest in between.

During the plane ride from Seoul to Tokyo, he reminisced about the big things God had done on the tour and then remarked:

"Jerry, Cliff, and I are going to take a boat from Tokyo to Honolulu, instead of a plane, because I feel a great need of getting alone with God. I have been giving out the message during the last two months. Now I want to spend much time in reading The Word and praying. I must sit at the feet of the Lord and have Him fill me again.

"Christ Himself felt the need of getting off by Himself for spiritual refreshment."

"You know," he added, "I feel a constant battle with the devil when I am preaching the gospel. When I finish a sermon, I seem to be drained of strength. By comparison, I can deliver a talk on international problems or civic affairs, and then sit down almost as refreshed as when I started. But it isn't that way when the gospel is preached. The forces of hell line up to do battle."

After the three had gone aboard the *President*

Cleveland, Paul Maddox and I went out to Tokyo Airport to catch the Pan-American clipper to Honolulu. Snow was falling heavily as we went aboard. We sat for about thirty minutes before the pilot announced that the snow was sticking heavily to the wings. He said he would make a run near take-off speed in an effort to blow it clear. If this failed, he said, the departure would be delayed until next morning.

It failed. We rode back into Tokyo through the heavy snowfall. Dawn revealed clearing skies and melting snow. The take-off was made without incident.

I was feeling very comfortable about the long ride, but lost my composure rapidly as Paul recalled grisly incidents of plane crashes around the world. One of the worst was caused, he said, when the propeller came loose and cut through the plane. My seat was next to the propeller and I couldn't take my eyes off the whirling air cleavers.

We landed at Wake Island, a tiny spot in the Pacific. "It's a miracle every time the navigator finds this thing," said the pilot.

Between Tokyo and Honolulu, travelers pass the International Dateline, making it possible to fly for a day and night and still arrive about the same time they left.

Billy chugged up seven days later. The meeting there had not been a part of the original itinerary, but in spite of hurried arrangements over 20,000 people gathered on a Sunday afternoon. Thousands of them responded to the message that had brought such incredible results in the Far East.

Afterwards, he spent several days relaxing on Waikiki and following a golf ball around the beautiful island.

A true account of the golf scores will have to be given by someone else, because I wasn't there. I was on a fast plane for Chattanooga, Tennessee, and a long awaited reunion with my wife and three little children.

During a thirty minute stopover in Atlanta, I was sitting in the restaurant, eating a piece of non-sacred cow, when a lady walked by. I had left her husband a few hours before in Honolulu. She was Mrs. Billy Graham on her way to Texas to talk about God at a big rally.

Billy had just finished a tour that would have killed some men, and here was his wife, serving as father and mother to their four children, flying to Texas with the same message.

You see, they believe that the message of Jesus Christ is the most important thing in the world.

RAINBOW IN BLUE JEANS

A man with much wisdom—my boss, Mr. Roy McDonald, publisher of The Chattanooga *News-Free Press* —once told me that the best parts of a trip were the anticipation of going and the joy of returning.

He was right!

It has proved true on all trips—a short motor journey to the Chattanooga suburbs or an airplane tour around the world.

I was privileged early this year to look forward to a globe-circling tour with my friend, Billy Graham, who is now as well known in Palamcottah, India, as he is in his native Charlotte, N. C.

It may have been possible for some to be dignified about such a prospect, but there had been too much turnip greens and cornbread in my country background for nonchalance about such an opportunity.

I couldn't wait!

The journey surpassed all expectations. Many memorable things happened—the flight past Mt. Sinai . . . riots in Bombay . . . the Indian newspaperman who accepted Christ at a press conference . . . man who walked 400 miles to attend meeting in Madras . . . crowd of 100,000 in Kottayam . . . Hindu holy man who fell on his face before God in Palamcottah . . . crowds at every airport . . . Billy's talk with Nehru . . . the filth of Benares . . . water tour of Bangkok . . .

incredible response in Manila . . . dinner with Generalissimo and Madame Chiang Kai-shek . . . lepers in Formosa . . . surging mobs in Japan . . . pathetic children of Korea, and many other unforgettable things.

The flight home was fast, but it wasn't fast enough. The plane finally reached Atlanta, and Chattanooga was only thirty minutes away. But the plane flew backwards most of the way.

In spite of this, however, the landing was made and I looked out to see two little boys and a girl standing there against the fence with their mother. Such an airport picture was nothing unusual to the other passengers, but to me the good Lord had wrapped up the rainbow in blue jeans.

After the long-awaited greetings, the little three-year-old boy chirped:

"Daddy where you been?"